About the author:

Marie Herbert was brought up in Sri Lanka, went to school in India and then attended the Central School of Speech and Drama in London. She has spent two years teaching English and Drama, five years as a researcher in advertising and public relations companies and also trained and worked as a transformational therapist.

She is married to the polar explorer, writer and artist, Wally Herbert, and has accompanied him (with their two daughters) on many journeys. These included living amongst the Inuit (the Polar Eskimos) of NW Greenland and the Saami (Lapps) in Norway and Sweden, as well as taking her young family on trips to Greenland. Her previous books, *The Snow People* and *The Reindeer People* were accounts of her experiences in the Arctic and her novel, *Winter of the White Seal*, was set in the southern Polar regions.

Healing Quest

A Journey of Transformation

MARIE HERBERT

RIDER
LONDON · SYDNEY · AUCKLAND · JOHANNESBURG

First published in 1996

1 3 5 7 9 10 8 6 4 2

Published in 1996 by Rider,
an imprint of Ebury Press, Random House,
20 Vauxhall Bridge Road, London SW1V 2SA

Random House Australia (Pty) Limited
20 Alfred Street, Milsons Point, Sydney,
New South Wales 2061, Australia

Random House New Zealand Limited
18 Poland Road, Glenfield,
Auckland 10, New Zealand

Random House South Africa (Pty) Limited
PO Box 337, Bergvlei 2012, South Africa

Random House UK Limited Reg. No. 954009

The extract on p. 34-5 is reprinted, by permission, from *How Can One Sell the Air? Chief
Seattle's Vision* ed. by Eli Gifford and R. Michael Cook. Book Publishing Company,
Summertown, Tenn.

Papers used by Rider Books are natural recyclable products made from wood grown in
sustainable forests. In addition, the paper in this book is acid-free/recycled/chlorine free

Typeset by Deltatype Ltd, Ellesmere Port, Wirral
Printed by Mackays of Chatham plc, Chatham ,Kent

A CIP catalogue record for this book
is available from the British Library

ISBN 0-7126-7451-9

To Pascale

CONTENTS

ACKNOWLEDGEMENTS

THE SUCCESS OF AN ENTERPRISE CAN BE GREATLY enhanced by the focus of people's good will – their encouragement acting like a web of invisible but tangible energy which is there to support one when things get difficult. The accomplishment of this book and the achievement of the events it describes was heightened by the knowledge that I had supporters at home, and others emerging on my travels, who wished me well – and to all these people I offer my thanks and gratitude. My agent, Cat Ledger of James Sharkey Associates, brought her perception and wisdom and enthusiasm to this book and the journey behind it, when my sense of its potential was still more than I could easily articulate. Judith Kendra of Rider Books was equally in tune with my aspirations and her courage in backing me helped to make the journey viable.

My friends, Dan and Jonolyn Weinstein provided a base for me in Jamestown and gave helpful advice on logistics. Al and Hanna Holt also offered their home as a base in Colorado, and found me a car with character which tested my confidence but which became a faithful companion and did all that Al had said it would. Dr James Gay and his wife Lilian provided me with guide books which are collectors' items, while Marguerite Adams showed me an example of true American hospitality with the loan of a cottage in the woods at Little Spruce Lake. Mimi Calpestri pointed me in the direction I needed to go at the start of my search, while Grandmother Spider introduced me to the ceremony of the purification lodge and taught me how to do everything in a sacred manner. Marina and Jenni were the first to welcome me 'on the trail'. Their generosity and kindness renewed my sense of trust and set the tone for the rest of the journey. My thanks to Peter and Julie Sabatino for their hospitality and caring and advice.

Some of those I met along the way have influenced the book even if they have not appeared in it. To them and to those who have not wanted publicity, I offer my gratitude. Karen Kolstad opened her home and her heart to me, as did Dennis and Marcia Miranda – they all have a special place in my heart. Jamie Sams in particular fired my interest and desire to learn more about Native American philosophy and spirituality, and I owe much of what I have learnt in the Medicine Cards and the Sacred Path Cards to her.

Thanks to Hanne Rotter for two memorable nights at the Grand Canyon, and thanks also to Roger Fertig and Fran Kuhn for the loan of their tent.

To Joseph Rael, also known as Beautiful Painted Arrow, I owe my blossoming intuition, and to Standing Eagle I owe my knowledge of how to create magic in my life, even if I do not always practice what I have learnt. The time spent with Talks With Bears and Maka will always remain a highlight of my trip, and a very special memory. To Speaks The Truth, I offer my gratitude for a deeply healing and wonderful time shared together. And to Debbie, Susan, Dian, Lynn and Sonya I send the biggest hug and my love. Most important of all, I want to thank my two soulmates, Wally my husband and life-partner, and Kari my daughter, for their tremendously loving and generous support, which allowed me the freedom to travel for six months, so that I could follow my heart and my destiny, find my new path, and heal what needed to be healed.

IN ORDER TO RESPECT AND PROTECT THE PRIVACY OF SOME OF the individuals in this book, some of the names have been changed. 'Crowhawk' is fictitious and in no way refers to any individual who may own or call himself by that name.

I wish to emphasize that what I have written refers to my own experiences and that if I have, unwittingly, misrepresented any aspect of Native American philosophy or way of life I should welcome advice about this, and any constructive comments. My intention in writing this book is to serve others who may be experiencing, or who have experienced, loss or sudden change in their lives – in the hope that the wisdom and grace that I received, and now share, may be a catalyst for their own journey towards wholeness.

I have where possible used the term Native American in the book to describe the original people who live in what we now know as North America. In certain cases, however, where the term Indian is used, as in Pueblo Indian, I take my reference from the indigenous people who answer to this name in their public persona, although they know themselves to be other than this. I would like to affirm my deepest respect for all the Native American people and offer my gratitude for the wisdom and insights gleaned from the beings I met along the way.

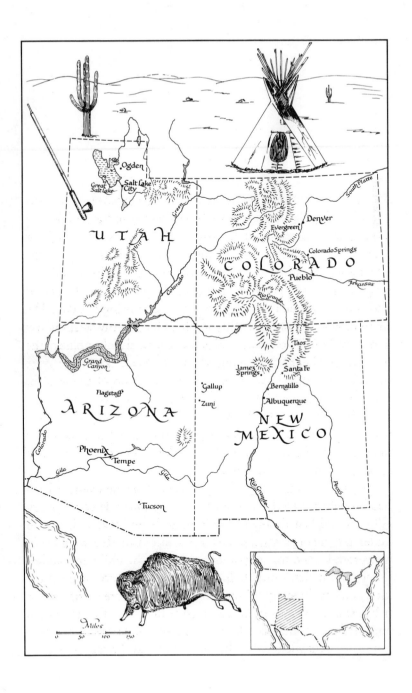

Ogden

Great
Salt Lake

Salt Lake
City

U T A H

Green

Colorado

South Platte

Denver

Evergreen

Colorado Springs

C O L O R A D O

Pueblo

Arkansas

Rio Grande

Grand
Canyon

Taos

Jamez
Springs

Santa Fe

Flagstaff

Gallup

Bernalillo

A R I Z O N A

Zuni

Albuquerque

N E W

M E X I C O

Colorado

Phoenix

Tempe

Gila

Gila

Rio Grande

Pecos

Tucson

Miles

0   50   100   150

INTRODUCTION

I T WAS MY THIRD DAY ON THE HILL; AS I SNUGGLED INTO MY sleeping bag I felt a sense of wellbeing and gratitude. For years I had wanted to visit this beautiful state of New Mexico, but nothing I had dreamed of matched the magic of the experience. I had been woken this morning by the sound of a songbird that had perched on one of the poles of the teepee. It had sung, it seemed, for me, blessing and praising the day. The smell of wood smoke and pinyon pine clung to my sleeping bag and to my hair. Though the top of the teepee, the clear blue of the morning sky beckoned me outside. I dressed quickly, feeling the night chill still on my clothes. In the tradition of the ancient ceremony that I was following, I would remain alone, and apart from the rest of the world, for four days and nights to 'cry for a vision'. This powerful ceremony, a healing quest overseen by a medicine person who is normally a healer and seer, is a method of seeking guidance in the form of a helping spirit.

As I sat brewing a cup of tea. I reflected on the events which had brought me to this extraordinary high-altitude countryside. When I had first thought of coming to New Mexico, it was to undergo a rite of passage; some form of initiation that would help me surrender the role of parenthood once the children had left home, and which would help me envision the next stage of my life's purpose. In many cultures, especially the more traditional or tribal, the transitions from one stage of life to another are noted and celebrated with specific rites of passage. These ceremonies not only acknowledge the change of status and circumstance in

1

the life of the individual, but they place the cycles of personal growth in a greater context. Change becomes meaningful, and even sacred, to be honoured and celebrated.

Change had been the one constant in a life of travel since I was four. I could handle its vagaries without undue effect. But with the prospect of my younger daughter, Pascale, going to a sixth form college away from home, I felt the first pangs of parental withdrawal. How would I spend my time when so many activities were no longer centred around a lively teenager? My other daughter, Kari, seven years older than her sister, would be completing university and looking for a job in London within the next year. To all intents and purposes, the active commitment of parenting was starting to decline. In large measure, I would be free!

But free to do what? And what would compensate for the challenges and fulfilment of family life? A career as a writer and then as a therapist in personal growth and development had occupied some of my time between the joys and chores of motherhood. I loved parenting, and felt that I had given it the best of me. My friendship with the girls enriched, enlivened and enchanted me. I was in no hurry for them to leave the nest, believing that every age and stage was a delight. But I also knew that sooner or later they would want to roam.

Just before the start of Pascale's year in the fifth form, about four or five months after her fifteenth birthday, I decided to do a retreat so that I could focus on the changes that would come into our life, and devise the best way to deal with the disruption to the familiar routine.

I had with me two packs of cards of Native American origin, psychological tools and sacred teachings which evoked one's intuition and helped one tap into one's gifts and potential. They were called Medicine Cards – The Discovery of Power Through the Way of Animals; and Sacred Path Cards – The Discovery of Self Through Native Teachings. Mildly divinatory, they had an uncanny way of highlighting what needed to be dealt with in one's life. Each card bore a shield with symbols which in Native American tradition carry specific lessons. I had spread the cards in such a way that they pointed to my life path. And the lesson that presented itself was of change: it said that I was coming up to a time of great transition and that I was in need of a vision quest.

'Vision quest': the phrase seemed mysterious and exciting, intriguing even. I read its lesson: 'The vision quest is one of the oldest tools used by tribal people to seek direction in life. Under the guidance of a medicine person (spiritual guide), the seeker is sent to a remote location to fast and pray for three or four days and nights. The result of this activity, which is called "Going on the hill" by the Sioux, is a fuller understanding of your place and pathway in the world. For many, the vision quest is a powerful rite of passage.'

As I read the text, I felt that was exactly what I needed – an insight into the purpose and possibilities of this next stage of my life. I would look for someone to take me on a Native American vision quest after Pascale went away to college.

I little knew how poignantly accurate the Sacred Path Cards were to become. Our beloved Pascale was killed just three months later on 4 November 1993. Beautiful Pascale, whom we had left smiling at the door only an hour before, I had found dead when my husband and I returned from a walk. She had been electrocuted in a freak accident – a one in a million chance.

In the wake of the tragedy the world turned inside out for the three of us who were left, my husband Wally, and my daughter Kari. So often we are told, 'Life goes on,' and indeed it does, but I believe we have each to choose the manner in which our lives continue after a tragedy. Initially, one is so shaken that one loses all sense of security and purpose. If it could happen to Pascale, who was such a radiant being with so much to offer life, then it could happen to any of us. We felt, initially, disorientated, rudderless, and totally unsure of the future.

Kari returned to university to complete her degree, which she did bravely and competently. Wally decided to travel and lecture. I could have accompanied him, but I chose otherwise. Each of us needed to find or own way through that door that Pascale had opened for us. When I say that one has to choose how to respond to tragedy or trauma, I mean that one can either look for its potential for growth, let it open one's heart and expand one's level of consciousness; or one can allow it to deaden one.

There is no arguing with the demands of destiny. I can only be grateful for the intense joy of those fifteen years, and the knowledge that I had no remorse or regrets for things done or undone. Now, however, I was not only facing redundancy as an active parent but also, because of the tragedy, really needed a vision quest to find the new direction my life should take, and to heal the past.

As I looked around the teepee, my eyes alighted on a picture of Pascale looking at me with beautiful clear green eyes. She was smiling.

CHAPTER ONE

Sweat Lodge

IN THE WEEKS FOLLOWING PASCALE'S DEATH, I MET Grandmother Spider, an American who had studied Native American traditions and ceremonies for many years and who had herself been honoured by being given the peace pipe by a Lakota Sioux medicine man. This accolade entitled her to officiate at births and deaths, and at the sacred purification rites of the Native Americans called sweat lodges. There was a gentleness to her, combined with strength, and kindness shone in her cornflower blue eyes. She had come to Britain to share her experience and knowledge; she offered dream workshops, Native American sweat lodge ceremonies or purification rites, and vision quests, which she had adapted for the British climate and temperament. A Jungian analyst as well, she was eminently suited to work with the psyche and its soul journeys.

The term 'grandmother' among the Native American people is a term of respect, a sign that one has become an adult. 'This normally happens around the early fifties. Before then one is just a learner!' She laughed as she explained it to me. I remembered that Joseph Rael, a part Ute, part Pueblo Indian, had written that women between thirty and seventy carry what he called 'descending light, of gifts brought forth from the heavenly plane'. I thought this sounded beautiful. It suggested that there is a wisdom, beyond that which we consciously acquire, which becomes available to women only in the later stages of their lives.

The name Grandmother Spider had seemed strange when I first heard it. But my new mentor explained: 'The spider is a sacred creature in Native American tradition, and is not to be feared. Spider is the symbol of infinite creative potential. It is said that she wove the first primordial alphabet and that she is the female energy of the creative force. Her eight legs are said to represent the four directions on the medicine wheel and the four winds of change. I feel privileged to be named after her.'

I instantly warmed to Grandmother Spider. When she knew that I was interested in going to America to do a vision quest in the Native American tradition, and my reasons for this, she invited me to participate in the sweat lodge she was running so that I could invoke the help of spirit through the ceremony, and become clearer about my intention. 'The sweat lodge is a powerful ceremony. Miraculous things happen at times. It could help your healing process, and will prepare you for your journey.'

I had often heard of these ceremonies but was afraid of taking part in case of being overcome by the heat.

'The sweat lodge is a sacred space,' explained Grandmother Spider, 'and it's sometimes called the earth's womb. It's a place to pray and to commune with spirit. I'm sure you'll be all right. And if you find the heat too much, you can always go outside. I won't make you suffer.' She laughed. Some medicine people were very strict, she told me, and didn't allow anyone to go out. But she felt a concession had to be made to people who did not have such ceremonies in their culture. 'Each part of the lodge has a special significance and when the Native people cut the willow saplings for the frame of the lodge, they make an offering of tobacco to the plant in gratitude for its sacrifice. Similarly, when they gather the rocks for use in the lodge, they again offer tobacco in thanks. Whenever they take anything from nature, the Native people first ask permission, and then leave an offering in return.

'The ceremony is something of a sacrifice. You give of your sweat in order that the people may live. You suffer the discomfort for the benefit of the people.' The people mentioned, as she explained, were not only two-leggeds, as humans were called, but also the standing people (the trees), the four-leggeds (the animals), and the winged ones and the creepy crawlers (the

insects). 'The sweat lodge is also an occasion for prayer and
praise, an occasion to give thanks.'

I approached the sweat lodge that Grandmother Spider had
prepared in a field on the edge of Dartmoor. A fire was already
burning in a shallow pit outside the entrance to the basket-like
dome, which the participants were covering with blankets. A
dark-haired, clean-shaven man of slight build, whom I imagined
to be in his late thirties, was tending the fire, on which he had laid
some porous-looking rocks. 'Only volcanic rocks can be used,' he
said when I remarked on them. 'Any other would explode when
heated. It's very important to remember that, as it can be
dangerous to use anything else.'

Grandmother Spider greeted me warmly and invited me to
help with covering the lodge, placing numerous blankets over a
dark tarpaulin. As things got under way, she took a drum from her
bag and walked in a circle around the area, beating a steady
rhythm, which I learned represented the earth's heartbeat. At
each of the four directions she stopped and appeared to be
praying.

This done she came over to where I was standing. 'Come and
sit on the rug, Marie, I want you to make some tobacco ties.' She
took out some different coloured cotton squares, seven colours in
all, and, cutting a length of cotton thread, showed me and several
others how to wrap small amounts of loose tobacco in each of the
squares before attaching them along the strand of thread. 'Don't
knot the thread or it'll prevent spirit from receiving the prayers.'

I was not the only one fumbling to attach the ties in the
prescribed manner, although in a short while we all became adept
at stringing them along with a deft twist to keep them in place. As
each person folded the cloth around the tobacco, he or she prayed
silently. I thought it was a wonderful way of anchoring one's
prayers.

I noticed that when Grandmother Spider made her own she
touched the tobacco ties to her forehead and heart before
attaching them to the thread. 'The seven colours,' she explained,
'represent the four directions as well as Mother Earth, Grandfather Sky, and the Great Mystery. You should string them in a

certain order: black, white, yellow, red, green, blue and indigo, which is the order the Lakota people use and, since this is a Lakota tradition, I don't see any reason to change it.' Different tribes, however, ascribe different significance to the individual colours and might arrange them in a different sequence.

'We need to go in now, the rocks are ready,' called our host. Grandmother Spider was the first into the lodge to bless it. She purified it with some pieces of sage, which she let smoulder in a shell. Sage or cedar is traditionally used by the Native people to purify a space or an individual. We stood in line to be 'smudged', as the purification rite is called. The smouldering sage was held near us and its smoke wafted all round us with the aid of a hawk's wing, a sacred object among some of the Native people.

I experienced a pleasant peacefulness as I waited my turn outside. The young woman smudging me coaxed me to turn with the touch of the bird's wing on my shoulder. She ended the process with a light touch of the wing to the centre of the forehead, saying, 'Mitakuye Oyasin', which means 'all our relations' in Lakota and reminded us that we are related to everything in the universe.

'Remember to bring in your prayer ties,' exhorted Grandmother Spider, 'and when you enter the lodge, come in on your knees. This reminds us to be humble in this sacred space. Also, as one enters the lodge, one repeats "Mitakuye Oyasin".' She pointed to a place just inside the entrance to the left. 'Marie, you sit there in the south, the place of the child.' I was to learn this was the place of trust and innocence, the place of growth and new beginnings.

I crawled in second but last, with someone on my right near the door flap. Grandmother Spider sat on the other side of the entrance, which she explained was always in the east. She wore a blue shift which accentuated the blue of her eyes and she grinned reassuringly at my questioning glance. 'You can hang your prayer ties over one of the frames,' she suggested, 'and then when you leave the lodge take them with you and throw them on the fire. That way our prayers are consecrated before ascending to spirit.'

Robin, her helper, handed in a bucket of water which she kept beside her. 'Ready for the rocks?' he asked.

'Ready,' she answered. 'Bring in four.'

As we sat in the dim circular lodge, we watched as each heavy stone came in red-hot on the end of a pitchfork. Grandmother Spider manoeuvred each rock into position in the shallow pit in the centre of the earthen floor with a deer antler.

'We bring in the rocks in fours or sevens,' she explained. 'These rocks are our grandfathers.' She handed me a shell with some pieces of cedar in it. Then she handed the pipe which had been lying on the altar outside to one of the other women. 'As the rocks are brought in, they are touched by the pipe to bless them, then you put a piece of cedar on the rock.' The sweet pungent odour rose crackling from the rock, filling the lodge with its cleansing aroma.

Once the first batch of rocks had been brought in, the flap was put down and we were plunged into a thick, warm darkness. Grandmother Spider explained that if we needed to get out in a hurry, we should shout loudly to her to open the door. Otherwise, if the heat got too much, we could lie down. Robin would be outside to guard the door and to tend the fire. I felt an indescribable sense of comfort and safety in the warm blackness of the lodge. The other women were strangers to me, but somehow all barriers dropped in the intimacy and sacredness of this special place.

It was explained that we would do four rounds, where we would pray both for ourselves and others. The first round would be to consecrate the lodge and to invoke the spirit of the west; the second to invoke the north and to pray for others; the third to invoke the east and to pray for ourselves, and the last to invoke the south, to close the space and to sing. Between each round we would open the flap. And if we needed to, we could go outside. Our celebrant explained that she would be pouring water over the stones from time to time, which would create a lot of hot steam. 'I'll give you some water to drink at the appropriate time,' she said, and she pointed to a cow's horn she kept for this purpose.

The warmth of the stones wafted over me and I felt myself

relax. Grandmother Spider invoked spirit and the presence of the first direction. In each separate round she called one of these archetypal energies, using musical-sounding names to identify them. From time to time, as the water was poured over the stones, waves of hot mist wrapped themselves around me. I felt a rightness in being there and a sense of gratitude for something I could not explain. Sweat lodges were not only a tradition of the Native Americans: the Celts had used them, and the Mayans. The Russians and Slavs had a sweat bath which predated Christianity, and these, alongside the saunas of Scandinavia, served a social function, besides being used at times for therapeutic treatment and ritualistic or esoteric rites.

I felt comfortably warm in the first round. At a demand from the medicine woman, Robin threw open the flap to let in a flood of daylight and fresh air. We had started the ceremony around 10.30 a.m., but once in the darkness inside, all sense of time disappeared.

As the flap descended once again over the entrance, and the cedar sizzled on the red of the rocks, we each had a chance to speak aloud what was uppermost in our hearts and minds. It was a time to reflect on what was important for us. What is shared in the lodge is confidential – which allowed for an intimate exchange of confidences that touched the heart as much as they revealed the speakers' aspirations or tensions. It was amazingly easy to pray out loud and as everyone did so, we seemed to deepen into ourselves.

A comradeship developed; the slight touch of a hand, the murmur of encouragement or sympathy from those around. Praying was never so natural. With each successive layer of hot rocks and steam the individual participants merged into a unit with a common aspiration. The desire for a peaceful world, the ending of oppression and suffering, and happiness and prosperity for all were what we asked for.

As we sang the Native American song of praise and gratitude at the end, the words seemed not to matter in their foreignness. We chanted them with spirit and felt purged and elated.

As we sprawled on rugs afterwards, we set out the food each had brought. Custom had it that a plate containing a portion of all the food was offered in thanks to spirit. The person who officiated was served next and then the fire-tender.

I asked Grandmother Spider how often one should go to a sweat lodge.

She shrugged. 'Some people do it twice a week, some people once a month, there's no set number. You do it when you want to.'

'And are they always similar to the one we've done?'

She laughed, exchanging a knowing look with Robin. 'What happens happens. Sometimes they're serene, and sometimes they're celebratory, and then again sometimes they can be very difficult. Occasionally people react to each other, not realizing that it is their own stuff that is being mirrored. Sometimes people are not prepared to look at themselves. Whatever they do not look at the sweat lodge will bring out. Nobody said it was meant to be easy. But things do change. This is a powerful ceremony and when you do it often enough, you'll experience many astounding things. There's a natural wisdom to the process, believe me. It's not to be treated lightly.'

As time went on, I learned that Grandmother Spider had been part of an organization in the States that arranged vision quests in the wilderness. 'I would love to do one of those,' I said.

'Well, why not?' asked my new friend.

A few days later Grandmother Spider offered to assist me if I should choose to do a vision quest. I had already decided I would go to the States to experience different aspects of Native American spirituality in its own home.

'If you like, I'll accompany you part of the way, and be your guide,' she offered. 'But you have to understand that I cannot give you a definite itinerary to follow. Vision quests have a life of their own. Things happen or don't happen for reasons that none of us can explain. Rather than you trying to plan out your journey in detail, you should let spirit guide you. But I can introduce you to some medicine people and you can take it from there.'

I was deeply grateful. Since I had made a commitment to do the vision quest, things had begun to fall into place. I already had a guide and some contacts.

CHAPTER TWO

Grandmother Twylah

I WAS DRAWN TO THE CATTARAUGUS RESERVATION, UPSTATE New York, by the desire to find a very special Seneca elder by the name of Grandmother Twylah. There were many wonderful stories about this exceptional lady. The granddaughter of a revered medicine man, she had choked and nearly died at the age of three, and had been resuscitated by her grandfather Shongo. This meant that his breath became her breath, symbolizing that she would carry on his teachings. He also prophesized that she would become a great teacher and that people would beat a path to her door to learn from her, but that her life would be burdened with some very hard personal trials.

I had come to the States to do my rite of passage in the form of a vision quest, as the Sacred Path Cards had encouraged, to usher me into that phase of womanhood when children no longer set the agenda for one's daily routine. I had heard much about Grandmother Twylah before leaving England from people who had studied Native American ancestral ways. She was regarded as a teacher's teacher and I was keen to meet this lady whose people, the Seneca, numbered themselves among the Iroquois, highly cultivated founders of a league of Indian nations that survived for centuries and which was a model for the present-day United States federal government.

It gave the Americans the example of elected delegates, as well as separate leaders for civil and military matters. The Iroquois have a reputation for producing great statesmen and, from what I gathered, Grandmother Twylah was a respected elder who spoke for her people, as well as being a visionary, and a remarkable character. Her fame extended beyond America and, as her grandfather had predicted, she drew students from all over the world to her home near Buffalo.

I had no idea where to look for Grandmother Twylah initially, not even which state she lived in. My surprise was great, therefore, when a chance remark at a faculty function at Jamestown Community College, where I was spending a couple of weeks with my husband, Wally, before starting my quest, indicated where I might find her. I was relying on old-fashioned providence to direct my way, which I had left very free after the first two weeks in Jamestown.

There was a rumour that this renowned elder, who had taught thousands of people the wisdom of her people's ancestral ways, had stopped teaching. A member of the wolf clan, she had released two white wolves into the wilderness, believing she was nearing the time of the great transition. I conjured up visions of an old, long-haired, weather-scarred crone, dressed in a long frock with Native jewellery, living deep in the heart of the forest, with wolves as guardians. I imagined her in a little wooden cabin, dismissing her wolves with fond but dignified farewells as she prepared herself for the inexorable decline of her energy.

In preparation for my visit I had bought some tobacco, remembering that it was considered good etiquette to offer it to medicine people whenever they did a ceremony, or whenever one visited. Tobacco was revered as a sacred plant and was used much in ceremony by the Native Americans. What I was to discover was that different tribes have different customs, and what is revered by one might be despised by another.

Locating the reservation was easy enough, and I felt curious and excited as I drove through a sunlit forested area to where her attractive white bungalow stood among the trees near several other timbered dwellings.

Few Native people live on their original homelands. Dispersed and relocated, mainly by pressure from white colonists, their Native soil was carved up and appropriated by the white invaders. Their grief was compounded by the fact that they shared a special relationship with the earth which they regarded as their mother. Every inch of it was sacred and needed to be treated with respect. To have the land torn from them was as injurious to their wellbeing as if they had had the heart torn out of them.

Dispossessed of the mother that fed them physically, emotionally and spiritually, many lived a miserable existence in the reservations on which they had been forced to live. Of the 50–60 million once living in what we now call the United States only around 2 million remain. In 1887 tribal ownership of reservation land was replaced by individual Indian ownership. While this safeguards some of the land for the indigenous people, ownership is an alien concept to the Native mind, but one they have been forced to understand.

They are, and always have been, first and foremost children of the earth and secondly its stewards. In most reservations the residents live in trailers or other humble dwellings, the ubiquitous abandoned cars that have become their trademark lying everywhere. On entering the reservations, one is immediately aware of a lower standard of living from that enjoyed in the towns and villages in which most white Americans live. It is not easy for the Native Americans to earn a prosperous income because their education does not equip them for the competitive nature of the white man's world, and they still meet with a certain amount of prejudice.

To my great joy, Grandmother Twylah was at home and welcomed me in for a chat. She explained that she should have been in hospital having an eye operation but that it had been postponed, otherwise we might never have met. She told me that she had been blinded once by the flashing lights of a diarama at a fair and didn't think that she would ever see again. During this time, however, she developed her other senses to a high degree to compensate. She also developed second sight, and once this was established got her own sight back.

This was not the only disability she had to overcome. She suffered deafness and recovered from it, was crippled and learned to walk again. 'All this,' she explained, 'is for a learning. It's all a lesson. Everything happens in life to teach you something.'

15

I liked her instantly. She was a petite woman, elegantly, if comfortably, dressed, with her greying hair held up softly with ribbon and slide. Very fair-skinned, with smiling eyes, she had a ready answer to questions, and a delightful sense of humour. Yes, she admitted, she had reduced her schedule to the minimum, but she still liked to teach an occasional weekend intensive. And people still visited her from all over the world. I gathered that she had given away her pet wolf (not wolves as story had it,) but this was because it took more energy than she could muster to look after.

'Why have you come to the States?' she asked me.

'I'm on a quest, because I lost my fifteen-year-old daughter, Pascale, just under a year ago. I feel I need some sort of rite of passage, both to heal the effects of this and to give me some direction. I'm treating the whole of my journey leading up to a vision quest as a medicine walk.' The latter, I knew, was one of the ways the Native people re-established personal equilibrium, and tapped into guidance from spirit which would manifest itself through the natural world. It normally involved a day alone walking in nature. I went on to say that I thought some new purpose might emerge in my life out of the tragedy, and that I had come to look at it as a form of initiation.

'You need to know yourself,' she said. 'Only by knowing yourself will you find the answers.'

I wondered, anxiously, did I know myself enough? If I didn't, by Grandmother's reckoning, I was going to have a fruitless journey.

'When is your birthday?' she asked.

'25 May.'

'You are essentially a seer; you have to create things for yourself as you can't be doing with other people's stuff.'

I was not sure about the first statement but I could relate to the second part of it. I dug into my bag for my offering to her. I leaned forward and held out the tobacco. 'I have heard it is customary to bring tobacco,' I said, offering it to her.

She tried to disguise her distaste, but an involuntary exclamation said it all. 'Ugh, I wish I knew who started that rumour.'

She looked so genteel and sophisticated a medicine person,

that I had to laugh at my faux pas. 'Sorry. Do you want me to take it away?'

'No, I'll just give it to someone who smokes!' she said.

I sensed that the Seneca tribe were more urbane than many other tribes. I also learned from Twylah that they regarded themselves as philosophers. I mentioned that I had already done some sweat lodges in England in preparation for my trip, but she interrupted me to explain that they were called purification lodges among the Seneca, and that they took great exception to the term 'sweat lodge'.

'Just because people sweat in them doesn't mean that they should be called that. Likewise, you wouldn't say that Christians went to church to drink and eat because they take communion.

I realized I was going to have to be very careful on this quest not to offend people inadvertently. No doubt I would learn as I went along.

'How did you come to start practising Native American spiritual ways?' she asked.

I told her that I had learned much from the teachings of Jamie Sams, her protégée, through working with the Sacred Path Cards and the Medicine Cards, and that I had been moved by the beauty and grace that she indicated were part of much of the Native American culture. Jamie had learned from the Seneca, Aztec, Choctaw, Lakota, Mayan, Yaqui, Paiute, Cheyenne, Kiowa, Iroquois, and Apache nations. Certain teachings were common to many tribes and were part of a universal ancient wisdom, and it was these which touched me and drew me to want to learn more about the Native way. They spoke about the sacredness of life and how everything in the universe is connected. They also taught that everything in nature is our teacher and our relative, and that each of the kingdoms of nature is equal and worthy of respect.

I very much liked the concept that we are all part of the sacred hoop of life, and I appreciated how the Native way encouraged and helped one to live in harmony with oneself and with the universe. I told her that I felt a strong connection to Great Spirit, which I learned resided within Great Mystery, and that I hoped to deepen this connection by participating in sacred ceremony. She puckered her brows slightly.

'What you need to focus on is Great Mystery. There is only *one* and that is Great Mystery, which is an energy contained in everything. It can't be divided. Religion put God outside of oneself. So we go outside of ourselves to find God when all the time we have Great Mystery within. If you say Great Spirit resides in Great Mystery, you have caused duality and separation. There is no duality. There is no separation. All is *one*. All resides in Great Mystery and Great Mystery resides in all. It is Great Mystery that you should pray to, nothing else.'

She suggested I come over for the next couple of days to study with her. 'You'll be much better prepared for your journey if you know who you are before you go searching all over the place.'

I could not help smiling at her forthright manner. She was a lovely lady, and I was only too delighted to be invited to spend some time learning from her. Hopefully, she would teach me something about myself that I did not already know.

Each tribe has a different way of describing the source and the story of creation. Twylah told me that she did not believe in an anthropomorphic god, which the term Great Spirit suggested.

'Great Mystery cannot be reduced to any one concept,' she explained, 'because it is an energy above and beyond as well as within all form.'

I was glad that she had spoken so freely, because it re-emphasized for me the difference in belief systems among the Native American tribes. The Lakota Sioux, whose philosophy seems to have influenced people's view of Native American religion in Europe, referred to Wakan Tanka, the supreme being, as all that is, both Great Spirit and Great Mystery, everything created and the act of creation itself. Similarly, the Sioux used the term 'sweat lodge', and it was on their ceremony that others based their purification rite. There were differences in belief even within tribes themselves. I could see that she was trying to encourage me to connect with the essence of things.

Grandmother Twylah advised me, as Grandmother Spider had done, that I should let my journey unfold rather than try and direct it, as this way I would be brought the lessons I needed to learn.

'You'll be all right on your medicine walk. Just look for the signs in nature. They're everywhere. And remember to listen.'

That first day I was shown an example of the teaching methods of Grandmother Twylah which reflected the easy naturalness of many Native teachers. I arrived as she was finishing breakfast, and already there were six other people who had come to visit her, like myself. One had even flown in from Australia. We sat around the kitchen table, and Twylah began to talk.

'People come here when the time is right,' said our host. 'All of us have been together before in some lifetime, and all of you have been Native Americans, some in more than one lifetime. You're all Rainbow Warriors, people who have agreed to help birth a new world – the Fifth World as we in the Senaca nation call it, which is the world of illumination, wisdom and truth. The Fourth World was the world of separation and control. We are moving from a masculine, patriarchal society, with all its aggression, competitiveness, ego, and exclusivity, into a feminine one of cooperation, community, sharing and inclusiveness.

Twylah then explained that the Native people had been made the keepers of an ancient wisdom. They had guarded and nurtured it through all the horrendous periods of oppression, never losing faith, despite times of utter despair. 'Some of the red race have chosen to incarnate as white in order to bring the message of hope and transformation to the rest of the world. Why do you think you have such a love for the Native American way? Why do you think our ceremonies resonate so much with you?'

The Fifth World, we were told, would come into being around the year 2013. Grandmother Twylah showed us a book she had written with Jamie Sams called *Other Council Fires Were Here Before Ours*, which she said explained the whole history of creation as her people understood it. She pointed to a picture of a rather misshapen stone, which she said was her medicine stone. 'There's my teacher.'

Through reflecting and meditating with this stone she had become the channel for the inspired message and prophecy which her book set out. Rocks and stones, she explained, held many mysteries and secrets; they were record-keepers of life on the planet.

They not only held stories of the past but could tell us about our future. 'We two-leggeds think we're so great,' she said derisively. 'We think we're the only spiritual beings in the universe.' But, she believed, our arrogance prevents us from seeing that other life forms on earth, such as animals, were equally as important as ourselves.

When asked about the Fifth World and its significance, she explained that there were seven worlds through which humanity had to travel in order to complete the plan of evolution and to 'return home'. So far the world had gone through three cataclysms, each of which had ended an era, because of the lack of respect people had shown for the earth and its creatures. The First World was destroyed by fire, as the Earth Mother sought to purge herself of the greed, hatred, arrogance, and manipulation that had distorted the world's original peace and harmony.

The Second World fared no better. It too fell prey to the ego's dark ambitions and was destroyed, this time by ice. The Third World, having still not learned the lesson, was destroyed by water. And finally we arrive at the closing stages of the Fourth World. It is frightening to think that, coming up to the twenty-first century, there is as much barbarism, racial hatred, religious bigotry, and greed as there has ever been.

Yet our world, instead of being destroyed, is to be reprieved. We have been given the grace to transform. The difficulty and trauma of that transformation are directly related to the quality of goodwill and cooperation that we can muster.

'The wars in the world reflect our inner conflict,' Grandmother Twylah reflected.

'The transition from Fourth World to Fifth World will not be without some dramatic changes,' she warned. Prophecy claimed that the Fourth World would be destroyed by a shift in the earth's axis, causing a polar displacement. But, as many spiritual teachers, including Grandmother Twylah, concurred, the physical effects of this manoeuvre would be minimized if enough people came into harmony with each other, and were aligned with higher consciousness. It could be likened to each one of us being a note, or tone, in a vast symphony.

'As long as we live in balance, peace, and cooperation with others, we are creating sounds of harmony. As long as we seek only personal gain we make a strident noise.'

Native Americans such as Grandmother Twylah teach that everything is connected. Modern physics supports this claim with people such as Fritjof Capra explaining this phenomenon with their own particular metaphor. Pythagoras understood that everything was made up of number (or vibration) and described stone as frozen music. He talked about the kinship we share with the whole of life. Hinduism shares the belief in sound (vibration) being the origin of physical manifestation with the Tiwa-speaking Pueblo Indians. Joseph Rael, a part Ute, part Pueblo Indian, says that within the vibrations of sound one might find the presence of the Great Mystery. Even Christianity claims that 'in the beginning was the word', word in this case being sound or vibration.

I was beginning to make a lot of connections that made sense to me.

Twylah talked a lot about language and how our words have power, and how they can also, wrongly used, disempower us. 'The word 'hope' has a hole in it. You can fall right through it. It has a negative energy instead of a positive one. In the Fifth World we should not use words such as 'hope', or 'try'. You can keep trying forever. Do what you intend to do.'

She spent most of the morning entertaining us with humorous stories and anecdotes, interspersed with homilies, and references to the cosmology of the Native Americans.

That afternoon, Twylah took us through a programme she had devised which taught us about the different animals and the lessons they had for humans. She was anxious to transmit as much of the teachings as possible; it was a rich diet of information and needed more time than was available to digest it. I was glad I had had Jamie Sams's version of the teachings in the Medicine Cards as an introduction to this idea, for it had presented the philosophy of the animal teachings in a simple and beautiful way, and I had had plenty of time to assimilate them. I understood that Jamie had spent much time learning from Grandmother Twylah and regarded the elderly medicine woman as her mentor. At the end of the day we all appreciated the importance of becoming more open-minded and sensitive to the world around us if we were to understand the language of other life forms in the way that many of the Native people did.

Twylah's home had become a sanctuary for many people over the years. People came to stay and study, sometimes working in the house in part exchange. A great camaraderie developed between her students, many of whom felt that visiting her was 'coming home'. Teachings are traditionally freely given and are reciprocated in different ways.

I could see that the day's effort had been a drain on Twylah. She gave me a hug, explaining how important it was to touch heart to heart when one embraced. I had indeed shared heart to heart with this special lady and I felt privileged and grateful to have been invited into her home under such circumstances. Before leaving, I took a stroll in her garden and was drawn to a large circle of stones which represented the medicine wheel, a place where specific sacred teachings took place. Nearby was an equally large circular building with a fire pit in the centre, which was used in summer for teachings. On the walls hung hawks' wings and dream catchers and other Native American artefacts.

As I was leaving, I noticed a young Australian healer standing near the door of the house. I had been chatting to her earlier and discovered that we both shared an interest in sound as a method of healing. I was just a novice in the field, while she had been working in it for some time. I had caught her looking at me searchingly, as if puzzling over something in my manner, and I felt I had to tell her that my quest had to do with losing Pascale.

She hugged me for an age, and then held my hands as she spoke to me.

'I wish I could have known earlier. I work with people who are grieving and can often bring them a message from the departed soul.' She closed her eyes for a few moments and said, 'Waybearer . . . Pascale was a waybearer. She is bringing you a new way.'

How many times I was to have this said to me. I thanked her, and promised to keep in touch. Then I left. Grandmother Twylah was too tired to teach the next day, so I spent some time with one of her students, going through some of Twylah's exercises to help one 'know oneself'.

The next several days I spent looking for an RV, a vehicle rather like a large camper van, with the help of my friends Dan and Jonolyn, with whom I was staying. My intention was to hire one of these mobile homes and to drive it to California to meet up with Grandmother Spider, and then continue down to New Mexico together, where we would contact some medicine people. But when I phoned Grandmother Spider in California to tell her of this idea, she said she had a family crisis and was not ready to receive me. Maybe I should go to the south-west on my own, since she knew I had a yearning to be in New Mexico, and she would catch up with me later. As it turned out, the cost of RVs proved prohibitive and I was persuaded that I would be much better off hiring one in New Mexico, as it would take several days' tough driving to get there.

The night before I was to leave, my host came in excitedly to tell me that a friend's sister lived in Gallup in New Mexico and that he was sure I could stay with her for a few days. 'I haven't seen this friend for ages, and I was just telling her about you and your travels when she volunteered the information that her sister, Jenni, would love some company. I didn't even know she had a sister in New Mexico. How about that for luck and coincidence!'

I answered that it smacked of synchronicity, and considered that maybe Grandmother Twylah was right when she advised me to let matters unfold. This was a perfect example of being in the right place at the right time, even if by proxy. 'Great Spirit does work in mysterious ways!' I thought out loud, and hoped a certain dear lady would not hear me.

CHAPTER THREE

Medicine Walk

I N MY ORIGINAL PLANS I INTENDED TO REGARD THE WHOLE OF my journey before my four days' intensive vision quest in the wilderness as a medicine walk. Medicine, I learned, in Native American tradition is anything that brings one into greater harmony with Great Mystery – the source – and all life forms. And although I did not intend to walk everywhere throughout my quest, the term 'medicine walk' seemed a suitable metaphor for the time I spent preparing for my retreat, and was indeed part of it. In a medicine walk, anything one meets on the way, any person, animal, or natural phenomenon is to be regarded as one's teacher.

There is something very significant about dedicating this time to connecting with the different kingdoms of nature, because everything is then lived more intensely. Among the Sioux, especially, the medicine walk was seen as a way of establishing a link with one's allies, or medicine helpers. To those sensitive enough to hear, the wind speaks to them; to those who perceive, the clouds show a picture. And to those who might think this far-fetched, the explanation of the Seneca elder Grandmother Twylah that everything is alive, and everything contains the same vibrant core (by which she means the same spiritual essence) would explain how spirit could teach and enlighten us through any one of its manifestations in the world around us.

I had planned to start my medicine walk proper once I got to New Mexico, but, looking back, I can see that my allies appeared as soon as I left England. Even before meeting Grandmother

Twylah, whom I felt to be an integral part of my learning, I had met Al and Hanna on my voyage across the Atlantic and had developed a close rapport with the latter, a blonde blue-eyed American lady of German birth, a bit older than I, who shared my love of nature and my fascination with human potential. I had told Hanna that I hoped to visit Native medicine people in New Mexico after a short while in New York State and California, and that I would be looking for an RV or large camper van to live in, as well as in which to travel.

'Why don't you come and stay with us after your time in New York?,' Hanna had invited. 'I might be able to find you a vehicle through some contacts we have if you've not already found one in New York.'

It was a generous offer but one I doubted I would be able to accept. However, when Grandmother Spider announced that the timing was not right for me to visit her in California, I decided that I would like to take Hanna up on her offer after all.

When I phoned Hanna, she could not have been more enthusiastically welcoming, and she and her husband Al met me at Denver airport after just a couple of days' notice. Her timber-framed home was cosy and attractive, set amidst forest and mountain meadow, with snowcapped peaks in the distance. Wild elk gathered frequently in the meadow in front of the house and dainty-faced mule deer were to be seen in the nearby woods. Hanna showed me photographs she had taken of the mountain meadows in spring and summer when they were ablaze with wild flowers. I knew that if I had been able to make contact with the medicine people in Colorado I would have been tempted to stay there.

I had two goals other than to do a vision quest: one was to learn from Native medicine people or shamans; and the other was to experience the land which shaped the lives and spirits of the Native people before the white invaders robbed them of it. It seemed to me that only aboriginal people, in the sense of primal people, the first to live in a place, developed this special relationship with the land. But before I could visit the places I wanted I needed transport, and that as soon as possible.

True to their word, my hosts had tried to find a vehicle for me but, as Hanna explained ruefully. 'The RVs are no cheaper to hire here than in New York. You could hire a modern car, but that would be expensive, or you could take something less likely to be noticed and broken into. We've already put the word out that you're looking for something modest to hire.'

I was grateful for their efforts, being rather apprehensive at the thought of setting off on my own without knowing if any of the contacts I had would be at home or even able to see me. In some cases I had only names, and no addresses, and in other cases addresses but no phone numbers. I had a limited budget for my travels and I didn't want to run out of cash before I had done what I came to do. I was relying on finding reasonable accommodation en route, and wherever I decided to settle.

I did feel sorry I was not going to have a travelling companion for some while. As if sensing my uncertainty about my travels, Hanna said, 'Why don't you invite your daughter, Kari, to come out for a couple of weeks? That way you can share the driving and see more of the countryside.' She grinned as she added, 'You won't be so nervous driving on the opposite side of the road if you have someone with you.' Hanna was as motherly as she was astute.

A few days later we went to the airport to meet Kari. Her delight at being invited out and our being together was matched by my own.

'You need to be together for a while,' said Hanna as she put an arm around each of us. 'Mum needs you to help her get confident with her driving,' she said to Kari, 'and you need fattening up before going back to search for a job.'

It was true we needed to spend a bit of time together before this next phase began in earnest for both of us. Kari had been so enthusiastic about my going off on my own, but we had had little time together since Pascale had died just to enjoy each other's company.

'Being here together is all part of the healing for both of you,' said Hanna. 'You'll each have plenty of time to be apart. just think of this place as your home, and enjoy being here.' She went off to turn on the hot tub which stood next to the indoor pool, and left us for a few moments looking out over the fabulous view.

'Wouldn't Pascale just love this!' exclaimed Kari.

I nodded. Pascale had always been a waterbabe and she would have relished swimming in such a wonderful setting. Remembering her, we gave each other a hug, and just then the strains of the singer Enya came drifting through from the room next door. Kari squeezed me extra hard. Pascale had loved this song. We had played it at her memorial service.

The memory of Pascale was very rich over the next few days as each of us remarked on things she would have enjoyed. At these times the impression of her was so strong we felt it like a presence. We both found ourselves, often, looking at things through her eyes, which always seemed to add an extra dimension. If we were not out exploring Colorado's mountainous beauty, we were getting our gear together for the trip we intended to make to the Grand Canyon and on into New Mexico.

Within a few days we had a tip-off that there was a car available which might just suit us. Kari came with me to have a look at it. It was a Dodge, twelve years old, which a mechanic friend of Al's had checked out. It had lain dormant in someone's garden for a few years but was deemed up to the job, after a few repairs. 'It's not the most recent model,' admitted its owner, 'but it'll get you anywhere you want to go in reasonable safety and comfort.'

What more could I want? I decided to take a chance on it.

As we loaded our vehicle, which had seen better days, Hanna cheered us on. 'The car's perfect for what you want. You won't look out of place in New Mexico or on the reservations,' she commented. 'You don't want to have anything that'll attract the wrong kind of attention.'

I agreed. Even if I had been able to afford a more luxurious model, I felt it would be safer not to look too prosperous, especially if I were to be driving on my own, after Kari left, in isolated rural areas.

Hanna ransacked her outhouse for camping things for us to take. 'I've managed to get you a tent,' she said. 'At least you'll be independent with that.' She fished out a spare ice box from the garage. 'You can fill a couple of freezer bags with ice from any petrol station; that way, you'll keep your drinks cool. Remember, you need to drink a lot at this high altitude. And don't forget, if you ever get lonely or want a bit of a break, you can come back here. Think of this place as your base.'

I could not believe how generous she was. The knowledge that I was always welcome there had an amazingly comforting effect.

Hanna had woken us at six o'clock and prepared a good breakfast which Kari and I had eaten sleepily. It would take us two days to drive to the Grand Canyon with all the diversions we wanted to make. I took the wheel with a mixture of excitement and anticipation. The route was downhill to begin with and the car cruised along nicely. It was light to the touch and I felt grateful at how easily I had managed to get hold of it. Things seemed to be working out remarkably well. At this rate, the journey would be a treat. But we had hardly been fifteen minutes on the road when my optimism waned. The car just did not seem to like hills and we had several mountain passes to get over. Even with my foot hard down on the accelerator I could not get the car to go more than fifteen miles per hour on the gradient and more often than not it could only manage ten.

We made an agonizing exit out of the district, taking turns at the wheel through staggeringly beautiful scenery. Mountains ringed vast plains. Wooded valleys led up to verdant slopes and there were always wonderful rocky outcrops to attract one's gaze. I journeyed back in time as I looked at the magnificent scenery, imagining those days before the settlers arrived when it was one vast hunting ground for the different tribes. Where they were empty now, except for the few herds of cattle, these high mountain prairies had been the home of buffalo.

We drove for most of the morning before stopping at a small roadside café in a rundown-looking area for a break. The car had bucked up slightly after an hour or so. Its top speed was 55 mph but this it could not sustain for any length of time. Most of the time it cruised between 35 and 45 mph. At this rate we would be on the road twice as long as we intended.

'Well, at least if the car's stolen it won't require a high-speed chase,' joked Kari.

It was wonderful being with her. In many ways I wished she could come with me for the whole journey, but I knew that was impractical. She had to find a job at home and I had to do this quest on my own.

'I can't get over the vastness of the place,' mused Kari as we drove hour after hour through broad vistas, up over mountain passes, and again through great rolling expanses. Here and there aspen groves, with their golden leaves, delighted the eye after mile upon mile of desert scrub. Isolated homesteads made me wonder about the lifestyle of their inhabitants.

'How do people fill their time in such desolate places?' I thought out aloud. When the Native peoples lived in the wilderness, most of them had lived in a community. In contrast, many of today's settlers live a very separate existence. Many Native tribes had been nomads before they were forced to settle in reservations. The Navajo, who had roamed a vast territory before they were restricted to Arizona and a small part of Colorado and New Mexico, are still fairly independent in spite of living on the reservation. Their voice is one of the strongest of the tribal nations.

'The thing about the Native Americans,' I told Kari, 'is that, like the Eskimo, or Inuit, they never owned land.'

'Didn't they?' Kari asked, surprised. She had lived with us in north-west Greenland for two years as a baby among a tribe who historically have been known as the Polar Eskimos. She had only a few recollections of the place, although these had been strengthened when we had later returned on holiday with two-year-old Pascale, when Kari had been nine.

'The houses belong to people,' I explained, 'but not the land.' In Greenland, the locals could put their homes wherever they liked, without owning the land.

'I thought the Native Americans lived on reservations,' Kari commented.

'They do. And strangely enough now, they do own land on the reservations. But the concept of possession is alien to them and is a legacy from the white man. There was a time when the Native Americans could hunt where they pleased. Now they can't hunt at all. There are no buffalo left except in private herds.'

I could not help thinking how so often tribal people were misunderstood, and how xenophobia created wars when these might have been averted. Many are the stories of how the Native people helped the arriving settlers with items of food when they were starving. But these tales are often overlooked when history is written, in favour of battles and skirmishes.

I wondered aloud to Kari how history might have been if the European invaders had been fewer in number, initially, and if they had had the chance to live peaceably among the Native people. If they had not sought to convert the Indians, if they had allowed freedom of worship, instead of trying to stamp out Native spirituality, which was inseparable from the rest of life, and if the newcomers had not been greedy for gold.

Gold, which the invaders would kill and die for, was not coveted by the Native Americans as a sign of prestige or wealth. Far from it. Like their cousins in South America they thought of gold as the excrement, or sweat, of the sun, and that sculpting it into an article of beauty was a way of honouring this spiritual force, and wearing it was an act of humility. The tribal people would only take what they could find on the surface of the earth, and these findings were likened to Mother Earth's fingernail clippings. Even today, the Native people regard mining as a violation of their earth mother. They take only the silver and turquoise which is above the surface, and they make an offering to show their gratitude in return. The silver and turquoise have protective qualities, and are used in a ceremonial context, as well as being worn for adornment.

'You know, the predominant view of the Native American was that he went round fighting and killing all the time,' I said to Kari. 'But few people know that there was a time when there was peace between the tribes, and when instead of killing or injuring someone to show their courage or manhood, the young men would do something called counting coup.'

'What's that mean?'

'Well, counting coup was an act of bravery whereby a warrior would steal something valuable from an enemy, like a horse, or a shield, or maybe a bow and arrows, anything that symbolized his opponent's power.'

'That sounds like a really good idea,' said Kari. 'But what about all the stories of scalping and massacres of women and children?'

'Well, for a start, it was the white men, the bounty hunters, who first started taking scalps to prove they'd killed an Indian. And second, there were far more massacres of the Indians and their women and children than there were of white people.'

'It just shows what misery the land holds beyond all its beauty,' commented Kari.

'Yes indeed.'

We both sat and mused between taking turns to drive, each of us lost in our thoughts but enjoying the presence of the other and the unexpected opportunity to explore this startlingly beautiful land together. I knew I would not have felt as relaxed if I had been doing this trip on my own. There was something about these vast distances that dwarfed one's sense of self.

Kari was beginning to fill out and look healthier. I had been shocked at the airport to see how thin she was since I last saw her six weeks before. It had obviously been pretty tough for her, with Wally and myself away. And yet we each had to do what was right for us at this moment. We each had our challenges. I wished I could have taken away all Kari's hurt and loneliness, but I knew also that it is through these tests that we grow. I had not imagined when I left home that Kari would have had such difficulty finding a permanent job.

My thoughts must have intruded on her for she turned to me and demanded, 'What are you thinking?' Her hazel eyes shone bright in her finely featured face which glowed with a soft tan. Her short dark hair gave her a gamine look. She had always been lovely to look at. I remember even when she was born looking at her in wonder, asking how such a beautiful child could come through me. I had a sense of being gifted with her, as if she were an old soul, and had always kept that sense of admiration as she grew up.

'You look at Kari with the eyes of a loving stranger,' my friend Pauline had said to me when Kari was an infant. As I looked at her now, I had still this feeling of joy. Each time I looked at her it was if I were seeing her for the first time.

But in reply to her question I admitted, 'I'm thinking what a great idea it is to have you here!'

She grinned and took a swig of water, before settling back in the seat with her feet balanced on the dashboard. 'This is what we like,' she purred. 'This is what we like!'

I laughed. It was something Pascale had always said when having a treat, and it had become a family saying.

The first day's travelling took us to Cortez, a small Hispanic town, where we decided to spend the night in order to get a good early start for our explorations the next day. We wanted to visit Mesa Verde, an ancient site of the cliff-dwelling Anasazi – the earliest inhabitants of the region – and would have to backtrack about nine miles to the turn-off. We were up at dawn. A beautiful pink light bathed the surrounding mountains as we set out. The road to Mesa climbs steeply and sinuously around a towering buttress. At each new elevation one catches spectacular views out across the plains. Mesa Verde is an apt name for this high plateau with all its trees and shrubbery. Here and there the deep green is broken by patches of russet from desiccated leaves. Mule deer, with their large ears, are well camouflaged, as ever they were, as they browse against the rocky slopes.

Mesa Verde is a maze of canyons and interlacing mesas. Home to the ancestors of the Pueblo Indians, as they are now called, this was a place unlike any other that Kari or I had ever seen. The people who lived there first were called the Basketmakers because of their extraordinary skill in weaving baskets which they waterproofed by lining them with pitch. Small woven bags were used for storage. They arrived around the year AD 1. Their way of life was simple: they grew corn, beans and squash on the mesa tops, hunted small animals and gathered wild foods, but over the centuries they developed their skills to a high cultural level. They built substantial homes which were clustered in small villages, first in caves and later on the mesa tops, and around AD 450 they began to make pottery, for which they are still remembered.

It being out of season there were no tourists around, so we had the place to ourselves. It was a gloriously sunny day with deep blue skies, and the air was crystal clear. We parked the car and followed the signs that led to the cliff dwellings. As we walked through the pinyon and juniper woodlands of this high plateau we both felt a strange sense of anticipation. The area opened up as we approached the edge of the tableland and we stopped at a steel fence that marked the rim of a broad, deep canyon and looked over. Together we both exclaimed with awe and delight. For there, nestling halfway down the sheer rock face opposite was Square Tower House, the extraordinary remains of a brick dwelling, built high off the ground into the wall of the sandstone cliff. In ruins now, it originally contained over eighty rooms and was quite the most unusual site for a dwelling that we had ever seen.

Why the inhabitants abandoned their homes on the mesa tops to live in such precarious surroundings as the caves and ledges of the cliffs is still something of a mystery. One can imagine the difficult access along the toe- and handholds in the cliff face. How did they deal with the aged or infirm? Mothers must have faced constant fear as they watched their youngsters playing within inches of the edge.

Looking at Square Tower House, which was only one of several remarkable cliff dwellings in the area, one was aware of a mythic quality which made it only too easy to believe that the inhabitants were magical and mysterious people.

'It is so good to do this with you,' Kari whispered, as she put her arm around my waist.

It made such a difference to the experience to share it with Kari. We spent the morning in a state of wonder as we visited several other equally dramatic locations. We stood in awe as we looked across the canyon at the great Cliff Palace, which housed as many as 400 people, and felt privileged to have enjoyed the timeless serenity of the place together, serenaded by the sweetest birdsong.

When we left Mesa Verde we headed as quickly as possible for the Grand Canyon where we were to spend a couple of nights. The journey took several hours. At times we were enchanted by the magnificance of the scenery, at others we drove mile upon endless mile through featureless landscape that numbed the brain and made our spirits restless. As soon as we entered Arizona the landscape became more desolate and arid. We stopped at the famed four corners, an especially sacred place to the Native Americans, where the Anasazi are said to have appeared first, around the time of Christ, and where you can step on the corners of four states at the same time: Colorado, Utah, New Mexico and Arizona.

We were tired and hungry when in the late afternoon we approached the outskirts of the Grand Canyon. Road signs had pointed to the nearby Navajo homeland with invitations to visit the shops on the reservation. The further we got from them the more urgent the exhortations to stop and buy became. We laughed when the last one said, 'Turn around. Go back. There are nice Indians behind you!' The Navajo reservation is one of the largest, but by no means do they enjoy the territory or freedom they shared before the settlers arrived. In many cases the tribespeople were forced to move off land that had been inhabited by their ancestors and were shunted to areas they would not have chosen to live in. I was reminded of the famous speech by Chief Seattle which so eloquently expresses the Native Americans' special relationship with and love of the land which the invader wished to buy:

> Every part of this country is sacred to my people. Every hill-side, every valley, every plain and grove has been hallowed by some fond memory or sad experience of my tribe. Even the rocks that seem to look dumb as they swelter in the sun along the silent seashore, in solemn grandeur thrill with memories of past events connected with the fate of my people, and the very dust under your feet responds more lovingly to our footsteps than to yours, because it is the ashes of our ancestors, and our bare feet

are conscious of the sympathetic touch, for the soil is rich
with the life of our kindred . . .

And when the last red man shall have perished from
the earth and his memory among white men shall have
become a myth, these shores shall swarm with the
invisible dead of my tribe, and when your children's
children shall think themselves alone in the field, the
store, the shop, upon the highway or in the silence of the
woods, they will not be alone. In all the earth there is no
place dedicated to solitude. At night, when the streets of
your cities and villages shall be silent, and you think them
deserted, they will throng with the returning hosts that
once filled and still love this beautiful land. The white
man shall never be alone. Let him be just and deal kindly
with my people, for the dead are not altogether powerless.

It was almost dusk when we arrived at the south gate of the Grand
Canyon National Park. We had only a few minutes to see the
canyon in the fading light, but it was enough to tantalize us with
its awesome grandeur. Nothing can prepare one for the magni-
tude of the place. We had an introduction to Hanna's friend who
ran the Red Feather Lodge and Holiday Inn deep in the heart of
the park, but it took us an age to find the place, after losing our
way several times in the dark. We were relieved and delighted
when we did eventually reach our destination, which was a great
deal more luxurious than I could hope to enjoy for the rest of my
trip. Our hostess gave us special attention and advised us to be up
early if we wanted to see the canyon at its most magical.

We followed her advice and rose early to see the canyon in the
morning light. We had to drive for a few minutes through a forest
of ponderosa pines to reach our vantage point along the south
rim. The vastness and beauty of the canyon is unimaginable. A
mile deep and 277 miles in length, it averages ten miles wide at its
heart. Great side canyons, lone buttes, and sculpted walls
blazoned with red and orange dominate the deep blue shadows
between them.

That first day, Kari and I decided to hike partway down one of the trails that led to the base of the canyon. It was exceedingly steep on the narrow path, and slippery in places, and I was aware how the canyon was the perfect symbol for the void, the abyss that my journey could take me into. The dark shadows of the deep gorges looked like mouths agape, ready to swallow the unwary. Entering the canyon, even the first few feet, is a heart-stopping experience. Suddenly one is made aware of one's lack of stature within the immensity of just one portion of this great rift. Far below, fellow hikers were reduced to ant size as they negotiated the serpentine trail with their packs, like some crumb offering, on their backs.

Our goal was a spit of rock one and a half miles down the seven-mile track. Kari strode nimbly ahead of me, occasionally stopping to make sure I was all right. The altitude and heat of the day parched the throat. But we had been well warned to drink plenty of water. As the day wore on the canyon became golden with splashes of bright orange. Several riders passed by on mules. The memory of a painful fall in the high mountainous region of Ladakh had prevented me from choosing this form of transport, but I envied the ease with which the mules made the ascent. We were five hours on the trail before returning dusty and desiccated.

It had been a great joy hiking with Kari. There had been a freshening of our bonding, which had taken on a new dimension after Pascale had died. A couple of days after the accident, Wally and I had shared some powerful moments with Kari during a meditation when Kari had seen Pascale go to Wally and me and give us a hug, and had actually felt this herself. On that very same occasion Wally had been given a vision of Pascale, ascending from her body in spirit form. 'Look, Dad, no scars!' she had said to him. He told us that her face, which had been scarred by the heat of the lamp falling against her, was radiant and without blemish.

We had always talked freely about Pascale since her death, and the three of us remembered her in a million ways. I knew the aching sense of loss I felt losing a daughter, but knew also that losing a little sister was a dreadful grief to have to cope with. I needed Kari's support to do this vision quest, and I was deeply grateful that she could allow me to take off to focus on myself and my own healing, without feeling excluded. She was a very strong young woman but I knew she had been really tested in this last year, having to deal with losing Pascale, then having to go on and finish her degree, and finally coping with setting up home in London and the unrewarded search for a job. I would miss her companionship and humour, and her sensitivity and affection when she returned to England.

Our patience was stretched to the limit the next day when an early start in the direction of Flagstaff was delayed because of trouble with the exhaust. We wanted to cover as much ground as possible early in the day so that we could get to Albuquerque in New Mexico, where we hoped to spend the remainder of Kari's time in the States. By late evening we still were no further than Flagstaff, having hung around all day to get the car fixed. A completely new exhaust system dug deep into my finances, but the car cruised along beautifully afterwards, so I had to admit it was worth it.

It would have been easy to let the delay dispirit us, but time was too precious. After booking into a motel we explored Flagstaff, enjoying the ambience of the university town, its student bars and restaurants. We had developed a taste for margaritas, the popular New Mexican drink, and toasted each other with blessings and good wishes for the next phase coming up in our lives.

Time seemed to have sped past. In the morning we realized that Kari would have just one more night before she flew back home. We needed to get to Albuquerque as quickly as possible so that we could do a bit of sightseeing later in the day. At least the engine performance seemed to have improved with the repairs; now, when I put my foot on the accelerator, it actually made a difference; the car drove like a dream; and the speedometer stayed at the maximum speed allowed all day.

Once again, we were awed by the variety and grandeur of the scenery. We saw the purple and vermilion tones of the painted desert, the weird and wonderful petrified forest, and the lunar landscape of the blue mesa. We saw magnificent mountains, towering buttes, and wind-sculpted rock faces. We saw signs pointing to ice caves and in the same locality, the long, tapering talus of extinct volcanoes. We saw so much to delight us. We pressed on, hardly daring to stop, so that we could make good going. In the silence that fell upon the journey as Kari dropped off to sleep, I felt a leaden grip on my heart. Tomorrow she would be leaving and I would be alone. The last week with her had been a magical experience. I ached at the thought of her going and wished she could stay.

Suddenly all the reasons for my journey rose to the surface, the need for a rite of passage to heal the past and to give a sense of the future. I was unsure how I would cope with the journey on my own, with its insecurity. I had contacts to follow up, but some of these were very tenuous, and might not even be still around. My movements were as much a mystery to me as they were to my family. All I knew was that I wanted to be in New Mexico. I wasn't even sure why I was so adamant about that. Perhaps because it was home to at least three medicine people whom I wanted to meet.

As we entered New Mexico, Kari and I cheered up. A high desert plateau stretched endlessly in every direction, always with mountains in the near or far distance, and always with the ubiquitous sage scrub providing a touch of green. As we approached the town of Gallup, which claimed to be 'the heart of Indian country', Kari suggested that we should look up the address of Jenni, someone who had offered to put me up for a few days. Gallup is a narrow strip of a town which extends a good fifteen miles along Route 66. At first glance it has none of the charm that its old town boasts, for all one can see are gas stations, restaurants, jewellery and pawn shops, and a few motels. A thriving industrial and mining centre, it owed much of its business to coal mining, and boasted the honour of holding an inter-tribal gathering every year in August. It is dominated by striking red rocks which were for me its saving grace, for there was nothing else, at first glance, to draw one to this featureless town in the desert.

We drove the length of its main street until very nearly the end, before recognizing any of the signs to Jenni's house. As it happened she was out, so I left a message on a card in her mailbox saying that I would call her from Albuquerque, where we were to spend the night, and from where Kari was to fly out the next day. Once in Albuquerque we hastily booked in to a hotel to be free to visit the historic old town. Modern Albuquerque is a bustling, high-rise, university city, which has an attractive residential area built in a charming Hispanic style.

The old town is built around a verdant plaza, dominated by an imposing Catholic church. It is a shopper's dream as there are so many wonderful things to view and buy. The Hispanic influence mixes wonderfully with the Indian.

All that evening and through the next morning, I felt tears welling up inside which I had great difficulty controlling. I did not want Kari's last day to be spoiled, but underneath the shared fun, I felt totally miserable. I could not understand the intensity of my feelings. I had been used to travelling on my own since childhood. The comings and goings, meetings and farewells, were commonplace – so why was I feeling such anguish now? Kari was not flying out till the afternoon of the next day, so we had several hours to return to the old town in the morning to enjoy its atmosphere. We explored lots of little side streets, had an ice-cream in the plaza, and posed for countless pictures.

In the car on the way back to the hotel, Kari reminded me of the car's quirks. She recited the measures I needed to take to check its various fuels, which she advised me follow, as a matter of routine, before I set out anywhere.

'Don't pick up hitchhikers, even if they're women, and don't sleep in the car,' she warned severely.

We filled in the hour before her departure with various bits of advice and encouragement to each other.

'I'm really glad you're doing this, Mum. I'm sure it's the right thing. I only wish Dad could find something equivalent to do. And even me. But this is your time, and don't worry about anything else.'

I was touched by the grace and maturity she showed. And then, suddenly, it was time for her to leave. I could barely see her through the haze of tears as I hugged her at the exit.

'You're trembling,' she said anxiously. 'Are you all right?' She looked at me, concerned. 'You'll be okay, Mum,' she comforted.

It seemed as if the roles were reversed for once. She was the adult and I was the child. I could barely speak. I did not know what had come over me but I felt bleak and forsaken. For several minutes in the car afterwards, I sobbed my heart out. I had never in my life felt so utterly and miserably lost and alone.

CHAPTER FOUR

Crowhawk

K ARI'S DEPARTURE LEFT ME FEELING DESOLATE. IT SEEMED
to trigger every feeling of loss that I had ever suffered.
Thoughts of Pascale came flooding back and the tears
ran in torrents. There was no stopping them. What on earth am I
doing here, I asked myself, and what do I do now? Suddenly the
prospect of travelling through New Mexico on my own seemed
totally disenchanting. Where there had been excitement before
there was now uncertainty, and where I had felt a curiosity and
kinship with the place there was now disinterest and alienation.
The joy of visiting a new city had given way to depression. It
seemed as if the traveller in me had vanished and all that was left
was the part that longed to be at home with my family.

It was a sobering thought to realize I could be so vulnerable,
and yet it was entirely to be expected. I had thought I had dealt
sufficiently with the grief that could trigger such emotions. But
there are layers and layers to the process of letting go of a beloved,
and when someone close to you dies suddenly and unexpectedly
you are left feeling bewildered. I knew that it was important to
accept one's vulnerability, for out of that comes strength. I also
knew that it is rarely the whole of oneself that is truly vulnerable,
rather the part that one has unconsciously identified with, but
that there are reserves of competence and courage one can call on
when necessary.

'You can't sit here crying all day,' a voice chided me from
within. 'The best thing is to get down to work. Go and look for a
medicine man or something!' I fished in my bag for my address

book. I was sure Crowhawk lived in Albuquerque. Crowhawk was a powerful medicine man and a good friend of Grandmother Spider's. I had written to him from England, telling him about Pascale and how I felt her death served as an initiation for the family. I told him about my desire to do a vision quest and hoped to be able to meet up with him and do some sacred ceremony with him. I remember the extraordinary way he had sounded when he phoned me. The voice had seemed spacey, the words spoken slowly and with long gaps between them, and as if they had a life of their own.

'He's often in another dimension,' explained Grandmother Spider when I told her about it. 'He spends a lot of time working in other realms.'

I had laughed when I heard this, for Crowshawk had sounded as if he were light years away, speaking from another planet. But he'd seemed friendly enough. I decided I would go and look him up. He had the reputation for being a great teacher and shaman, and officiated at important ceremonies such as the Spirit Dance and had taken part in many Sun Dances, where the men are pierced in the chest with a thong which is attached at the other end to a pole representing the Tree of Life. The participants dance without food and water for four days and nights before throwing themselves back to release the grip of the thong. On occasions dancers have come close to dying in this great sacrifice which they do 'that all the people may live'.

I must have searched for about an hour before I found his home in the less affluent part of town. The drive had raised my spirits and I was excited and curious at the prospect of meeting him. I had no phone number, so I could not warn him of my visit, nor could I be sure that he would be at home. I passed several humble dwellings before I chanced upon his. A couple of dogs barked from behind the wire fence and I hoped they would not be able to get over it. One of the most frequent complaints of travellers is of dogs attacking them in settlements. On closer inspection, I discovered that both of the apparent monsters yapping at me were no more than pups. That was comforting! The front door was very slightly ajar so I presumed someone was home. I knocked but got no answer, and it was several minutes before I could make myself heard. Then a man of about forty came to the door, casually dressed. His hair was pulled back off a round, swarthy face and tied in a ponytail that was rather sparse. His brown eyes looked at me, mildly curious.

'Crowhawk?' I asked.

He nodded.

'I'm Marie Herbert, a friend of Grandmother Spider. We've spoken on the phone.'

He puckered his brows as he tried to recall the occasion, then he smiled. 'Ah yes, come in.'

He paused, as if to let me explain my visit, and I began with the fact that I had just said goodbye to Kari, and that I was on a vision quest because of what had happened to Pascale. And with that I lost it. No amount of effort could stop the tears that once again sought release.

My host looked away with a mixture of concern and embarrassment, which I was beginning to feel myself. And then, as abruptly as it hads started, I managed to put a lid on my outpourings and I was normal again. Crowhawk responded to my efforts to be chatty by first asking if I would like a drink, and then telling me about the greatest event that had ever happened to the Native Americans, namely the birth of a white buffalo calf in Wisconsin in 1993. 'This is as important to us as would be the second coming of Christ to you.'

I had heard of Miracle, whose birth was as auspicious as his name implies. To Native Americans, and most especially the Lakota people, it meant the fulfilment of a prophecy that would herald a spiritual rebirth for the entire race and an era of peace and unification.

'It's a very exciting occurrence,' explained Crowfoot. 'It's really an answer to prayer. And so some of the dances, such as the Spirit Dances that we used to do, are no longer needed, since the purpose of them was to invite spirit to come into our lives. It may even be that we need to create new dances of celebration and thanksgiving.' Crowhawk's face shone with the delight he felt.

'We don't even know yet what the implications of the white buffalo calf are, all we know is that it's a sacred omen.'

The story of white buffalo woman is sacred to the Lakota Sioux. The story goes that one summer many years ago when the people were starving and there was no game, two young warriors were sent out to hunt. On the way, they spied a beautiful young woman coming towards them. One of the men felt lustful towards her and tried to grab her. He was immediately consumed by a cloud of snakes and reduced to a heap of bones. The other young man realized that they had come upon a powerful spirit and returned to camp to tell the people that he had seen a holy woman who was on her way. When the woman entered the camp of the Lakota, she gave them a sacred pipe and taught them how to pray. 'With this holy pipe, you will walk like a living prayer,' she said. Before she left, she told the people that she would return. And as she walked away, she rolled over four times and was transformed into a white female buffalo calf. After that day, the Sioux took care of the pipe and buffalo were plentiful.

'I have no dance ceremonies planned at this moment,' replied Crowhawk when I asked about his programme. 'But I'm doing a healing sweat lodge this weekend near Santa Fe which you can come to.' He went on to explain that he was doing it for a young boy who had been bewitched. I looked startled and he explained that a Mexican 'Brujas', or sorceress, had cursed the youngster and made him ill. 'What they often do is to create something which affects the breathing so that the person dies.'

I felt a sense of great unease as he talked about it. My reason for coming to the States to do sacred ceremony with medicine people was because I found their form of spirituality beautiful and gentle. The negative form of spirituality, or black magic, was not something I wanted to to get mixed up in.

'I don't think I am ready for such a ceremony,' I croaked.

'On the contrary,' said Crowhawk, 'I think it'll do you and your daughter a great deal of good.'

I quizzed him about the term 'sweat lodge', saying that I had been taken to task for using that expression when I visited

Grandmother Twylah, and that she'd said I should call it a purification lodge.

He hesitated before replying and explained, 'It's real name is Inipi in Lakota, but people call it many things. Some people refer to it as the womb of the mother, other people call it the cave of the bear. Most people follow the tradition of the Lakota in the lodge. In the west we call it a sweat lodge or a purification lodge. What matters is not so much what you call it but that you give it respect.

'The lodge is a sacred space. In our tradition we believe everything has life. So when you go into the lodge you are going into something that is alive. These days the lodges are covered with blankets and tarpaulins, but in the old days they would be covered with buffalo hide or the skin of the bear. Both these animals carry a very powerful medicine.'

The buffalo, I knew, was in many ways the most sacred animal, as it represented the major source of sustenance for the plains Indians. Every part of it was used. I had been told that it symbolized abundance, prayer and praise – it reminded people to be grateful.

'The bear hibernates in the winter, and comes out as if newly born, thereby representing birth and death. Each time you enter the lodge you go through a little death of part of the ego, and each time is a possibility to be reborn.'

I asked Crowhawk why it was that some people said the lodge represented creation in microcosm.

He pondered the question. 'Maybe because it uses the four elements, earth, air, fire and water. All the kingdoms of nature are represented in it,' he said, 'the plant, the animal, the mineral, the human, and of course the spiritual.'

I thought hard to understand what he had just said. And then I knew what he meant. The frame of the lodge is made from willow; rocks, referred to as elders or grandfathers, are used to hold the heat; feathers, antlers, and horn are used ceremonially; while we humans attend the lodge and call upon the spirits of the ancestors and of the four directions to be present, along with Great Mystery. All was contained within Great Mystery and

Great Mystery was contained within each thing. I knew there was more to the magic of the Inipi than we had discussed, but I did not want to take advantage of my host's time any more than I needed. I rose to go.

'Where are you living? asked Crowhawk.

I explained that I had made contact with the sister of a friend of a friend, who had offered to give me a room in Gallup for a while, but that I would need an alternative place as a base.

'I know it can get expensive travelling around. These people might be able to help.' He gave me a scrap of paper on which he had written the address of some friends of his, on whose land he would be doing the sweat lodge.

'They're very good people, you'll like them. They sometimes let out a room, or teepee, to people. They might be able to put you up for a while.'

It was time to leave. I had phoned Jenni in Gallup the night before and she had said she would be in at 6.00 p.m., and that I would be welcome any time after that. It was a great relief to have somewhere to go for a few nights. But the thought of retracing my route for a couple of hours or more, along the road I had come with Kari the day before, did not enchant me. There was something lifeless about Gallup that disturbed me.

I said goodbye to Crowhawk and he gave me directions to get out of town. Once out of Albuquerque the scenery opened up to vast stretches of desert scrub, ringed with mountains. It was arid, it was stark, it was beautiful really, but once again I felt a cloud descend on me and I was in tears. Part of me could observe my response to things while another part of me floundered in it. This did not bode very well. I had never acted this way before, but my therapist's training told me I would just have to ride it through. Whatever it was that had brought it on so suddenly, and I was sure it was Kari's departure which had somehow triggered much of the unresolved shock and grief from the last year's events, it would take its own course, and I would just have to accept it as part of my vision quest. I did not have to beat myself up because I felt lonely and dispirited.

Looking back on such experiences one can laugh at them and

wonder what all the fuss was about, but when one is at sea with turbulent emotions, every new challenge seems threatening. I think also I was affected by having to backtrack. I had a sense of anticlimax, almost of failure, as though something special had been aborted. I felt relegated, as if I were moving away from 'civilisation', which Albuquerque represented, into the back of beyond, which Gallup represented. It was unnerving. I knew it was all to do with my state of mind but, the fact was, yesterday I had been driving along this very road, marvelling at the scenery's magnificance, and today when I travelled along it it looked empty and barren.

I drove for an hour before I felt any respite from my confused emotions. The gap I felt in my soul at Pascale's absence was mirrored by the huge empty spaces of the landscape I was going through. I was perplexed at the size and depth of my uncontrollable grief. Had I not already dived into the abyss of my emotions in a significant gesture to clear them? Just a couple of months after Pascale had died, I had been given a challenge by a spiritual teacher named Carl Shapley, who had urged me to pick up the gauntlet which grief had thrown down and do battle with it. He suggested that for a period of forty days I should retreat into the wilderness of my inner space and there find the joy which I believed I had lost. Each day I was to meet life with joy, whatever its challenge, and each evening I was to review the day with gratitude.

'We do not own children or even beget them,' he said, echoing Kahlil Gibran's *The Prophet*. 'We are loaned them or serve simply as a channel, or vehicle, through which a soul, one of God's children, can incarnate. Sometimes a soul will only need to bounce off earth – maybe take one or two breaths before leaving the planet – to experience the density of this earthly incarnation. Pascale is resting now, and needs to do so, but if you need to contact her for comfort that will be allowed. Think of her as being in the next room, not as if she has left the house. Where you experience loss, while understandable in the circumstances, it is something you have allowed in. There is no separation, and it is this message and learning that you need to embody during those forty days.'

I had entered wholeheartedly into the 'experiment'. One way I found to deal with the ache in my heart was to imagine she was asleep in another room, and that I had tiptoed in to see her resting peacefully. Inwardly I would tell her that I loved her, as not a day had passed in her life but I would say, 'You know how much I love you?' 'Yes, I know,' would be her soft reply. Thinking of her resting I would send a beam of love from my heart to cocoon her. This helped. I was worried at times that wanting to feel her presence might intrude on her space or even hold her back from continuing her soul journey. But I was led to believe that I could tune in to the bigness of Pascale, her higher self, without jeopardising her journey, as long as I kept true to my intention that she be free. I could still give my love to her for comfort and protection, which she could transform into energy to do whatever she needed to do.

'The challenge put to you is to be open to experiencing your multi-dimensionality, your soul self and that of Pascale. If you do this faithfully, if you allow only God in, and monitor and reject negativity, you will experience levels of awareness never before felt, you will have an inner experience such as you have never had before. Be sensitive to the light and to the light growing in you: this releases loved ones to get on with their appropriate experiences. Your special relationship with Pascale will move into a transcendental position. You can become a teacher to others as you become more sensitive to light and more in touch with your own light, more and more in touch with dimensions beyond the human.'

Day by day I monitored my feelings faithfully, transcending some, engulfed by others, all the time making that special effort to be in touch with joy, and especially the joy that Pascale represented. The discipline of ending each day focusing on what I had to be grateful for was extraordinarily uplifting and healing. In those first few weeks of losing her, at times I was so consumed with a sense of loss that I wanted to be with her. Life on earth held no attraction. But called upon to take stock and be grateful, I saw that joy re-entered my life. Some days, facing the task of sorting through her things, I would be awash with emotion. While clearing through her papers and course work for school, I could see the things that moved and directed her; already, aged fourteen, a sense of life purpose beginning to unfold, concern for the downtrodden and abused. Her heroes were Steve Biko and Martin Luther King, her ambition to own an orphanage and somehow work with whales and dolphins at the same time, and sing.

As my mind recalled one episode after another of bittersweet memories, another wave of emotion blurred my vision. And yet those forty days had shriven so much, and restored so much of my own selfhood.

I stopped at a roadside café to freshen up. I didn't want to arrive at my host's looking miserable, but I wanted to get there before it got dark so that I would recognize the landmarks to Jenni's home. One thing I did not want to do was to turn up as soon as she got in from work.

When I did arrive, I was met at the door by a small, dark-haired woman in her forties. She smiled warmly. 'Welcome. Treat this place as your home.' With that she showed me through the bungalow to a pretty bedroom. 'I've got a meal cooking, so just relax. A glass of wine?' I sank on to the sofa and was immediately pounced on by an over-exuberant pup. 'You're obviously a soulmate,' called Jenni from the kitchen. 'She doesn't take to everyone that comes.'

I quelled the affectionate face-lick as I reflected on how kind people could be. Here was I, a complete stranger, and Jenni received me as if I were an old friend.

'It's so good to meet you,' toasted Jenni over a beautifully cooked steak.

'It's good to be here,' I responded, and I realized that, for the time being, I had nothing to worry about. I was being well looked after. That evening we chatted about all manner of things. Jenni knew the purpose of my journey and had already tried to set up some meetings for me with some Native Americans she knew.

The following morning Jenni was up at dawn and out of the

house soon after. Her job was managerial and she worked a good hour's drive from Gallup. Many of the staff were Navajo and there was one in particular she wanted me to meet. She suggested that she call for me at midday and drive me to her office in the afternoon, where she would introduce me to some of her Navajo colleagues before taking me to Canyon de Chelle, a well-known beauty spot and a place sacred to the Navajo and Hopi. I spent the morning sorting through my gear and taking a stroll.

When Jenni returned at midday she made a sandwich lunch, then we piled into her Jeep for the run to her office. As she drove, she pointed out areas of interest and talked about the Navajo whom she had learned to love.

'They're very proud people and don't rush to make friends, but once they've accepted you they're the best friends you could have – fiercely loyal and protective.'

I was introduced to Marina, her personal assistant, a stunningly beautiful Navajo woman in her late twenties. 'Pleased to meet you, Marie,' she said as she clasped my hand with a gentle but firm grip, her eyes smiling. She had long dark hair and a striking figure which was complimented by an elegant dress.

'I've heard about your journey and your interest in experiencing some of our ceremonies. Maybe you'd like to come along to a sweat lodge tomorrow evening at my nephew's house?'

'I'd be delighted,' I responded enthusiastically.

'That's settled then. See you tomorrow,' said Marina, 'about seven?'

As we drove off, Jenni remarked with some surprise, 'She must really have taken to you. I've never known anyone be invited to one of their homes that quickly. Count yourself lucky.'

She spoke almost admiringly and I could not help feeling pleased. The invitation was totally unexpected and all the better for that. I did wonder how I deserved such luck.

We drove through wonderful forests and lake areas which Jenni said were part of the Navajo reservation. 'They're one of the largest and most influential tribes. They're also matriarchal, and descent's traced through the mother: the women own the property.'

She told me how misunderstandings had risen historically between whites and the Native Americans. 'You've probably heard of the expression "an Indian gift"?'

I had but did not know what it meant.

She explained. 'Let's say an Indian gave a white person a horse as a gift. If after a while he saw that that person wasn't using it, then it was assumed he didn't need it, so the Indian would take it back. This of course wasn't understood by the whites and caused a lot of trouble. The Indians have a different system for dealing with property than we do. Lots of things are shared communally and so when they followed their custom and used things which the whites believed belonged to themselves, all hell broke loose.'

We passed a house on the high mesa which had the beginnings of a construction outside, with flags hanging from the poles. 'They're getting ready for a Yeibichai,' Jenni explained. 'It's a ceremony which lasts nine days and is accompanied by a great deal of chanting and dancing. There're many reasons for having a Yeibichai: it might be to cure sickness, pray for rain, or for anything else they need.'

I could not help thinking how varied was the Native Americans' approach to the spiritual. There was no one religion shared by all the people. Each tribe had its own creation myth and special ceremonies.

Jenni told me that the Navajos did not like planning things long in advance, for fear that wayward spirits might interfere and mess things up. 'They don't even like calendars for the same reason.'

I was aware of being in territory where spirits can sometimes get in the way of one's good intentions. When Jenni's offices were first built, the video surveillance cameras taped someone burying something in front of the main door. This caused great upset and fear among the Navajo workers who believed that the place had been bewitched and that it would be unsafe to work there.

Sensitive to the mood, Jenni arranged for a medicine man, respected by the workers, to come and deal with the situation. He uncovered a virtual 'witches brew' of black magic items which had then to be carefully disposed of in the correct manner. He followed this by blessing the building in a special ceremony. Only then were the workers prepared to carry on with their duties. I told Jenni that I thought she had acted very sensibly in the circumstances. 'You have to honour people's customs here,' she declared, 'or you'd never get anything started.'

Jenni decided to take me through the heart of Navajo country to Canyon de Chelle, 'The way tourists don't go,' she confided. I was stunned by the incredible beauty of its sculpted rocks. Rising like obelisks were two rocks which she said are sacred both to the Hopi Indians and to the Navajo. She pointed to one of them which she said is called Spider Rock. 'That's where the Navajo's creation myth begins,' she explained. Spider Woman, I remembered, wove the web of life out of her womb. I recalled some of the red rocks I had seen with Kari on our way to the Grand Canyon. They had looked like columns of figures waiting to be born. In every rock wall you could glimpse faces emerging and disappearing with the changing light.

As I sat in reverie, looking out over the canyon to the panoramic views receding in the distance, Jenni found a warm rock ledge and lay down on it, eyes closed.

'I rarely get the chance to relax like this,' she murmured. 'I hope you stay around for a while.'

I didn't know what my movements would be. I was looking for something, I didn't know quite what. There was some ceremony, some happening, some rite of passage that I was searching for and I did not know where I would find it. I told her about my hopes to do a vision quest. I had written off to do one with some people who organized them in California, but I had not had confirmation of the dates or if they could take me.

She asked more about it.

'Well, it's a bit like a pilgrimage, only in the tradition of the Native people they'd go into the wilderness on their own, fasting for four days and nights, to seek an answer to their problems or some new direction to their life.' I was seeking both a healing and a new direction, although I was concerned about the fasting since I felt very ill if I did not eat.

Jenni looked at me quizzically. 'You're going to be in trouble then, aren't you?'

I shrugged my shoulders. The vision quest, which was usually preceded by a purification lodge, and maybe even ended with one, was a more powerful ceremony, I believed, than a traditional Western retreat. The powers that are invoked in a vision quest have been invoked for thousands of years, long predating Christianity. Somehow the idea of the vision quest deeply appealed to me, almost as if it was resonating with an ancient part of my psyche which could be satisfied only by a ritual which derived from a spiritually orientated world view, rather than a dogmatic one.

I believe we need to honour these spiritual 'preferences' as much as we honour our music preferences, or any other significant choice we make for our happiness and wellbeing. The journey of the soul, I believe, spans many lifetimes, and during these lifetimes we may have lived in different parts of the globe, sometimes taking the gender of female, on other occasions male. To my way of thinking, many of us have experienced being part of another religion in different lifetimes. We learn something from each of these lifetimes and from each of our experiences; but some forms of spirituality have more heart in them than others, and from what I had learned about the different forms of Native American spirituality, many of them were full of heart. I had felt called to find the vision and healing I needed in a Native way, where the manner of communing with the numinous involved the whole of one's being living and acting in a sacred way, rather than confining the sacred only to one's prayers.

'So, will you sleep in a tent?' asked Jenni.

'Well, I believe I'm meant to sleep under the stars. Exposure is all part of it, you know.'

'Why?' she asked, puzzled.

I had not been asked that before and so I had to think for a minute or two. 'Well, I suppose you get in touch with nature better that way,' I replied.

She did not look convinced. 'You can freeze your butt off in the desert at night,' she mused. 'Seems like too much hardship for me. You sure it's necessary?'

I felt decidedly uncomfortable about the conversation. Was it hardship for hardship's sake, or was deprivation really important for the experience? I did not know.

'Are these Native Americans who are leading it?' she asked.

'No, but they've had a lot of experience and they're very highly thought of.'

She said nothing for a while. 'Maybe there are other ways, other people doing it, which are less arduous.'

If there were, I did not know about them, so until I did, I would have to follow the lead I had.

She got up to leave. 'Let's see what Marina has to offer,' she said pointedly. 'She seems to have taken you to her heart and, believe me, that's a compliment.'

That night, I lay in bed for hours without sleeping, a condition which was to plague me for the rest of the journey. Jenni's comments and implications worried me. But she did make me wonder if there were other less taxing ways of achieving the same result. I did want to do a vision quest, but was I really up to four days' exposure without food? That was not the only challenge: the desert was home to scorpions, snakes and spiders. Deep inside me, I had an irrational but firm belief that I would somehow be protected from them if I went into the exercise with the right attitude. After all, the main intention was to tune in to nature and to the Great Spirit, so that with the necessary precautions one could avoid confrontation with any dangerous wildlife.

It was seven when we arrived at Marina's the next evening. She lived in an attractive modern bungalow not far from where she worked. There was a fire in the living room and the place was comfortable and cosy. Two little children played in the front room near Marina and two older ones were in another part of the house. I learned that the latter were relatives of Marina's and brought up by her as was the way among the Navajo. Those who were more affluent or successful bore the burden of their extended family.

Before driving away, Jenni volunteered to pick me up in a

couple of hours. I was really touched by her generosity. Marina drove me in a very smart van to her nephew's house where I discovered the sweat lodge was already in progress with a group of men.

'You will be able to go in later,' said Marina's nephew, who looked as old as she. It was a good half-hour or more before it was our turn to go into the lodge.

Marina explained, with some surprise, that there would be only the two of us in the lodge as her nephew and his wife would be unable to attend. 'I thought there would be more people,' she said apologetically. 'It means that I have to be the one to lead the ceremony, and it'll be the first time I've done that.'

'That's absolutely fine by me,' I answered.

While we were waiting for the men to vacate the lodge, Marina asked me about my family and my reasons for being in the States on my own. I explained and she asked me to tell her more about Pascale. I described Pascale's love of animals and her efforts to safeguard their rights and how she wanted to adopt orphans when she grew up. Marina's eyes filled as she listened.

'I can't imagine what it must be like to lose a child,' she said.

She told me about herself and her family. 'Among the Navajo we always introduce ourselves with the names and clans of our grandparents,' she told me. 'That way, you know who you're related to, and then if you're in trouble the different clans will help you. I always introduce myself that way, even if I am giving a presentation to strangers, for then if there are any of my clan in the audience they'll introduce themselves afterwards. I feel at home then.'

I changed my clothes and then followed Marina outside to where a domed tent, covered with blankets, stood next to a shed in the small back garden.

'Where's the tobacco?' Marina asked her nephew.

'I'll bring some out,' he called.

I pointed to the tobacco I had brought as an offering. Marina rolled a cigarette with the tobacco her nephew brought and I realized that not all Native Americans use the pipe for such ceremonies, as I had imagined. I could see that Marina was mildly disappointed that her nephew was not there to explain things to me, but I reassured her that I already knew about the ceremony and had participated in several in England.

'If you're ready, we'll go in,' she invited. She crawled in first and motioned me to follow. 'Sit there by the door and then you can go out if you need to.' She placed a bucket of water beside her in which had been placed a cedar brush to purify it. I noticed her puffing madly at the cigarette to keep it lighted. Her conversation came in bursts. 'I'm smoking this to bless the place,' she explained. 'You know tobacco is a very sacred plant, and we smoke it whenever we do any ceremony. It connects us to the creator.'

I was reminded of a saying that pipe smoke was the path of prayers to heaven; presumably cigarette smoke was the same in the same context.

I had brought a towel with me to sit on, but I was glad there was already a piece of carpeting placed around the fire pit for that purpose.

'I'll bring in the rocks when you're ready,' Marina's nephew shouted from inside the kitchen.

'Ready now,' called Marina, and he brought a few on a shovel to add to those already in the pit from the previous men's sweat. He closed the flap and we were plunged into a warm darkness. I could see the glow of the cigarette darting about like a firefly.

She began to speak in the darkness in a soft, lilting voice. 'Dear heavenly Father, Creator, we ask you to be here with us in the lodge today. I'd like to welcome Marie who has come all the way from England. Heavenly Father, Creator, bless her, ease the pain in her heart.' She poured water over the stones, letting a welcoming steam envelop us. 'Dear heavenly Father, Creator, I pray for her family that she has left behind, may they also be blessed. May they be safe and comforted by you.' She went on to pray for Pascale and for the success of my journey. 'Heavenly Father, I pray that Marie will learn about my people, the Navajo, and understand them. May she discover what she came to learn and tell it good when she gets home.' She prayed hauntingly and poetically that I would be healed of my loss and that I would understand the purpose of Pascale's death. Her voice trembled with her heartfelt emotion as she spoke about Pascale and all the projects she had been involved in. 'Heavenly Father, Creator, help Pascale, who touched so many people. May her vision be carried on by her friends and other people.' She talked of how painful it must be for a mother to lose a child, and I could hear her weep, as the wisdom of the sweat lodge worked its magic to raise to the surface those emotions in both of us that needed to be purged.

She splashed water on the rocks and more steam rose, cloaking us in its fierce temperature. The accumulated rocks gave off a powerful heat and I was relieved to put my head outside the flap when it was opened. A beautiful young woman, of the Seminole tribe, had opened the flap and came in to join us. More rocks were added to the pit in the middle. Marina introduced us to each other. And we began another round. Each of us was asked to speak about ourselves and why we were there. Marina passed the bucket of water to me so that I could begin the circle of prayer and pour the water on the rocks when each had spoken. It was a lovely gesture of sharing.

The young Seminole woman spoke, invoking spirit in her native tongue before adding, 'First I would like to welcome Marie to our country. I wish that she remember that even as she has lost Pascale, so at that moment, somewhere, a baby would have been born to illustrate the cycle of life which continues.' Her voice wavered as she prayed, 'I ask that she be healed of her great hurt. What greater hurt has a mother than to lose her child? I pray that Marie learn to know herself and her true purpose, and that she receive the vision she seeks.'

My heart opened as she prayed for me. Each prayed out loud for themselves, for each other, and for their family. When this was done, each prayed for something better for the world. The heat was blisteringly uncomfortable and the newcomer and myself had to lean part out of the lodge for air. Still Marina sat there in the heat and spoke.

As I listened to her words, spoken so directly from the heart, I felt as if I were listening to poetry. There was a cadence to her language, a flow and repetition. It was like listening to a bard reciting some favourite verse. I prayed for the intentions both had shared with me, and prayed also that they would remember the grace and beauty of their people, and the wisdom which it had been their gift to share; and that they be not downhearted when they met misunderstanding and intolerance. The young woman opposite me spoke of the sadness of her people, of the hardship some of the elderly suffered, and of her hope that both white and Native American would be united in peace and harmony. It was an evening of shared tenderness and intimacy. I felt emotionally cleansed and nurtured by the experience.

CHAPTER FIVE

Talks With Bears

I PHONED GRANDMOTHER SPIDER FROM GALLUP TO TELL HER about my plans to do the sweat lodge with Crowhawk, and she was delighted.

'That's wonderful. It should be such a special occasion.' She went on to say that circumstances had arisen that made it difficult for her to join me. 'I'm aware of the promises I made to you, and I'm still committed to helping you in any way I can. But some urgent family matters have arisen that require my attention.'

I could hear the strain in her voice. 'As things stand at the moment I don't think I'll be able to join you. If you feel confident enough travelling on your own, it would release me to deal with things here.'

'Sure, you do whatever's necessary,' I responded. 'I'm absolutely fine.'

'This doesn't mean that I'm giving up on you. I can still be your guide, albeit from a distance. I think of you constantly,' said Grandmother Spider, 'and I smoke the pipe for you every day.'

I was touched and grateful that she did this for me. A spiritual guide holds the energy for a person on a vision quest, but does not need to be with her all the time.

To smoke the pipe for someone is to honour them in a very special way. It is a unique way of praying for them. The pipe represents unity, the balance of the male and female sides of one's nature. The tobacco that is placed in the bowl is dedicated to all the kingdoms of nature and, with this act, becomes representative of these. The smoke represents the spirits of all the things that were put into the bowl and is a direct prayerful link to the creator. By smoking the pipe for me, my friend could link in to me from a distance. Her prayers would protect and guide me.

'Let people and events come to you, Marie. Spirit knows better than anybody what you need. Trust that everything is happening as it should,' she encouraged me.

I heard her news with a mixture of surprise and confusion. I hoped she was all right, but it was a shock to realize that she might not be able to join me. And yet, I felt a curious excitement and a sense that things were all happening in the correct way. Maybe I needed to travel on my own. Grandmother Spider had been an inspiration and encouragement at a time when I needed that. Her enthusiasm had fired my own and given a boost to my resolve. She would have been a great companion, but I was beginning to feel that I should do the journey on my own, since only that way would I be able to focus on the process taking place within me. Only by being alone and apart from the normal events of my life could I make the inner journey to find my strength and purpose.

Snowstorms had blown throughout the day, casting a pall over both the surroundings and our spirits. Added to which, I felt exhausted from lack of sleep. Jenni decided to look at my car which she said had leaked oil all down the road and into the garage: the newly concreted floor had a big black stain on it! I decided that since I could do nothing with the car myself, I should get on with some housework as my contribution to the running of the household. Jenni complained that there were several important components loose under the bonnet, which she had now screwed on tightly, but that the car looked unreliable and worthless.

'You should return that heap of junk and get your money back. There's an important valve which looks on its last legs. It could last three miles or blow at 3,000. Either way, the car's a hazard and the sooner you get rid of it the better.'

I listened glumly. The car had been checked out by a good mechanic and I knew that my friends would not have let me have it if it were unsafe. But there had been a large tube loose under the bonnet which I had seen myself, and I had been obliged to replace the entire exhaust system. I could not afford another car, but nor could I afford to be stranded in this one in some remote part of the country. I felt I had to take it on trust, to a certain extent, even if I were worried about it. Meanwhile the weather was worsening in Gallup and heavy snow was forecast for Santa Fe. I phoned the friends of Crowhawk, to see if the sweat lodge was still on, and got directions on how to get there. At the moment, the weather was beautiful with them but, yes, they knew snow had been forecast.

The next day was the anniversary of Pascale's death. We had agreed as a family that we would contact each other about this time. Wally had just arrived in Montevideo on his way to the Antarctic. Kari was in London. So I phoned both of them. It was wonderful to hear their voices. We agreed that we would all tune in at the same time the next day to think of each other and of Pascale.

I was up early on Friday before Jenni left for work.

'There's black ice on the roads,' she told me. 'You shouldn't leave until midday or later. There's a five-hour window in the weather this afternoon when you should be able to get through.'

I knew I would need at least four hours or more to get to Santa Fe and find the place, but I could not bear to wait half the day before leaving and decided to go at 9.30. It was bitterly cold. I had to inch my way out of Gallup, but once away from it the roads were clear. Hurray! I was delighted to be on the move.

I was glad I had left early. The desert landscape looked beautiful, its prairie grass rimed with snow. As always, my eyes were drawn to mountains or rock: lone buttes, or vast ranges of red wind-sculpted rock. I felt nourished by the warm tones of the rocky heights and was exhilarated to be travelling. From time to time, I talked out loud to Pascale as if she were in the car with me. 'Well, we made it, Pascale. I thought I was going to be stuck in Gallup all day, but I got out of there pretty easily . . . I can't believe it's been a year since you left: sometimes it feels like yesterday and other times it feels like years. And sometimes I really can't believe you've gone at all. I really can't believe it. Oh, Pask, you know how much I love you, don't you? You know how much I love you . . .'

My thoughts drifted to Wally and Kari. We had a very strong connection to each other. I imagined a triangle of light linking the three of us, with Pascale in the middle bombarded by our love.

Driving into Alberquerque, I negotiated my way through the busy traffic to the old town quite easily. It looked festive with its chilli ristras hanging from the flat-topped buildings surrounding the open square. They were crusted with snow, a bizarre touch. The plaza, an attractive Spanish-style square, full of shops selling colourful and exotic wares, was crowded with visitors. In one of the open arcades some Native Americans had laid out their silver and turquoise jewellery on the ground. Small in stature, brown-skinned and dark-eyed, with black hair, they waited patiently for people to buy their goods.

The time we had agreed to do a meditation for Pascale was approaching, so I decided to go into the church in the plaza, reasoning that it would be the quietest place to reflect. It was very peaceful in there. It felt good to be able to tune in to the family, knowing they were thinking of me too. I knew both of them would find a place where they would not be interrupted to do a meditation linking up with me. We had done many such meditations together, sometimes in the same room, sometimes in different cities, although never so far apart as this, with Kari in London, Wally in South America, and myself in New Mexico. I lit a candle and reflected on Pascale and her short life. She had been so active in the womb just before her birth, doing a complete turn and turn about, again and again, as if she could not make her mind up to be born. Who was it who said, 'Souls waiting to be born are infinitely more frightened than those about to die'? With the complication of Pascale pushing against the umbilical cord, the doctor had decided to do an emergency caesarian. Wally had been up in the Arctic for six months by then, and when Pascale was three months old I had taken her and Kari, aged seven, up to the wilds of east Greenland to rendezvous with him. I have a wonderful picture of the babe, looking like a little Buddha, asleep on Wally's lap as he nods asleep over her.

A couple of years later, when the family visited north-west Greenland in 1980 for three months, Pascale had her second birthday, which was celebrated by the Inuit with a meal of boiled seal and walrus. Like Kari, seven years previously, Pascale had tucked into the seal with relish, charming the Inuit with the words she had learned of their language. It must have reminded Kari of the years previously when she too had stolen the scene with her good looks and spiritedness. The bonding between Pascale and myself was such that it seemed as if the umbilical cord had never been cut. So often in her early life we seemed to be pulled by the same strings, and when I stepped forward, Pascale would step forward at the same time and we would collide.

As I looked back over the years, I could feel the same poignancy I had felt as she responded to the challenges of growing up. The joy and heartache of friendships; the mastery of shyness, uncertainties and fears; the struggles and occasional failures, the achievements and triumphs alongside the growing confidence and the competence to do so many things. What had I sensed in those last few years, what urgency or impulse had made me tell her every day, 'You know how much I love you?'

As I thought of her now, and touched into that special radiance that was always hers, I imagined I was sending a great beam of love towards her, and had a great sense of her presence. As I was about to leave, I caught sight of a woman praying fervently in Spanish. Her face looked at the statue of the Madonna despairingly and my heart went out to her, understanding something of her distress.

I decided not to linger in Alberquerque. At the Tourist Office, where I went to buy a map of Santa Fe, the woman attending me warned, 'Snow is forecast but you should be okay if you leave immediately.'

Thoughts of Pascale vanished as I negotiated my way through the heavy traffic out of the city. People drove aggressively and fast, and I had to concentrate hard not to be drawn off course into the many slipstreams that led back into the city. Once out of the metropolis, I drove for over an hour through wonderful scenery, past brush-covered dunes and open plains towards snowcapped mountains beyond. I was still in awe of the vastness of the open spaces between cities. Only in the Arctic had I seen such great expanses.

One of the hazards of travelling alone, in a strange place, is the likelihood of misreading directions and arriving somewhere one did not want to be. Worse than this, I suppose, is arriving in the wrong place because one had failed to read the directions. When I set out for Santa Fe it was in the misguided belief that I needed to cross it in order to pick up the road that led to Talks With Bears and Maka's home, where the sweat lodge was to take place. My excitement was great when, cresting a steep rise, I saw the outline of a city swathed in the shimmering blue-purple of distance in the foothills of towering mountains.

The joy of arriving in this attractive city of adobe buildings was much dulled after an hour's fruitless search for my route onwards. Harried by drivers who were anxious to get home, I navigated maladroitly through the maze of streets and one-way systems as the late afternoon sun blinded vision and obscured the street signs. Normally when I am in a tricky situation in a car I put on my hazard lights to buy me time, but to my dismay my vehicle did not appear to have them. Without them to gain me grace, the homebound drivers assumed the worst of me, and mouthed abuse as they hammered their horns. The worst offenders, I noticed, were women.

I was beginning to feel very hot and bothered when I noticed a petrol station ahead, and pulled in to regain my composure. It was nearly sunset and, from experience, I knew how difficult it is finding a strange place in the dark. It was only when I reread the directions that I realized I had no need to come to Santa Fe at all. Talks With Bears and Maka lived south of Santa Fe, on a route I should have taken about ten miles back.

I decided the best solution was to phone Talks With Bears and get fresh directions. A man's deep voice answered the phone: Talks With Bears. He sounded so wonderfully calm and reassuring when I told him my predicament.

'Don't worry,' he encouraged, 'it's not difficult to find us.' He spelled out directions which I scrambled to write down before my change ran out, but I had only half of the route explained before the phone went dead.

By the time I had rushed into the petrol station to change some money, someone else had commandeered the phone. I waited impatiently for my turn again but to my relief Talks With Bears had awaited my return call and he painstakingly repeated his instructions. Eventually, I had a string of landmarks to guide me to his home. He even offered to come and look for me if I did not arrive within a certain time, and asked for the description and number of the car. 'If you get lost, wait at one or other of the landmarks I've given you, and I'll find you.'

That's the kind of man to do business with, I said to myself, and decided I liked him immediately.

My journey took me the length of Cerrillos road, a main artery through Santa Fe which is at least fifteen miles long. The setting sun shone directly into my eyes, obliterating road signs, and making the early stages difficult. 'I can't say I like this,' I said out loud to Pascale. Perseverance brought me finally to the right road and I knew that all I had to do was keep going. I had driven for about half an hour when I noticed two gypsy caravans parked on the verge of the road, with about twenty donkeys tethered nearby. There was something quaintly reassuring about this. I was so enchanted by the sight of them that I nearly overshot my turning – a dirt road that wound into the country for miles. Fortunately it was still daylight or I would never have found the turnoff – the entrance to it looked like a private drive.

As soon as I left the main road I seemed to enter another world. Great rocky outcrops rose on one side of the road, a vast mesa reached towards mountains on the other. Talks With Bears had told me to look out for a couple of teepee frames near a big rock. I drove for about three miles into wilderness, awed by the emptiness of the place and its wild beauty. I noticed the teepee poles, and then my eyes were drawn to the rock nearby, and I was transfixed by it. It glowed warm and pink and magical in the evening light. Huge and rounded with dips and curves and alcoves, it housed the statue of a Buddha in one of its many niches. A sleek blue-eyed husky dog came to meet me, wagging its tail, unlike the other dogs I had met on my travels that barked or growled. This seemed significant somehow, and a great relief.

A figure, with the presence and solidity of sculpted rock, stood with arms folded waiting for me. He was a handsome man in his forties, with glossy black hair drawn back across his head in a ponytail. His dark eyes greeted me with a mixture of warmth and curiosity.

'Talks With Bears?' I queried through the open window.

'And you're Marie?' We shook hands.

'What a fantastic place this is,' I enthused. 'That rock – it's just stunning.'

My new acquaintance shrugged and asked amicably if I had any luggage I wanted brought in. I pointed to a couple of bags, and followed him along a narrow path between the house and a cluster of feathery Russian olive trees that had turned a beautiful autumn russet. He led me into the kitchen where his wife Maka, an auburn, blue-eyed, fair-skinned woman, greeted me cheerily, before asking if I would like a cup of tea. I felt immediately at home. 'Sit next to the fire,' said Talks With Bears.

There was a strong presence about him that might have been daunting had it not encouraged respect. The serious cast of his expression was softened by a ready smile when he relaxed, and he was forthright in asking about me and my reasons for travelling. I told him about my family, and admitted that today was the anniversary of Pascale's death. I felt comfortable talking so intimately with these strangers.

'What do you hope to get out of your vision quest?' he asked, and listened attentively as I responded.

'I think, primarily, I would like a healing of the events of the past year, and I would like to get some sort of feeling about where I go from here. My future work. I feel Pascale has opened a door for each one of us in the family, and that we each need to go through that door alone and in our own time. And possibly the three of us will find something different on the other side.'

He nodded as he listened to me. 'We're glad to have you here,' he said, looking at me as if I were an old friend.

And, with that, I felt an extraordinary sense of wellbeing and warmth descend on me.

Talks With Bears showed me through the house, which he had built in and around part of the rock to reveal a textured, weathered wall in his living room. The natural curves of the rock were augmented in places to provide niches for ornaments. He used an artist's eye to create an ornamental feature out of something plain, or utilitarian. A tiny arched window not only provided diversion in the plain wall, but also framed an interesting aspect of the view.

'How long have you and Wally been married?' asked my host.

'Coming up to twenty-five years this Christmas Eve.'

He gave me a look which seemed congratulatory. 'You know, sometimes after people lose a child, the couple divorce. You know why that is?'

I didn't, although I had heard that it happened.

'The reason is that the two people look to each other to supply the joy that the child gave them. They don't realize that they've got to find that joy for themselves and not rely on someone else to provide it for them.'

It was a sound bit of wisdom, and I wondered if he thought that maybe Wally and I would do the same.

'I can see how people would think that,' I answered. 'In my own situation, I feel that the only way to honour Pascale is to embody her joy. She was a very joyful person.'

Talks With Bears nodded. 'It's a good way.'

'Of course, it's not the only way,' I insisted. 'There are many ways of honouring a person, but it's an important way for me.'

As the evening wore on, the subject of relationships deepened into a discussion about many different issues. 'The Indians are very tolerant people in general,' my host informed me. 'We're taught not to judge a person until we've walked 10,000 miles in their moccasins. The Indians didn't hate the white men when they first came, they tried to help them. And, you know, no Indian would persecute another tribe because they had a different religion. The Indian respects everyone's right to their own spirituality, they're very tolerant of this.'

I learned that Talks With Bears had strong opinions on most things, which rarely conformed to standard beliefs. He had a passionate love for the earth and wished for nothing better than to enjoy the fruits of the planet, lifetime after lifetime. Many Native spiritual teachers talk about the journey of the soul through various lifetimes on earth. Each life is a learning, they say, made up of lessons for soul growth. Eventually, when we have reached a state of wholeness, we will return to Great Mystery, the source. Some Native American creation stories indicate that people came from the stars, notably the Pleiades. And when all the earth lessons have been mastered, it is to the stars that the soul will return.

The Dakota people, the Creek Indians, the Osage, the Iroquois, the Hopi and the Cherokee, all have myths relating to their origin in the Pleiades. Whereas the Navajo, when they emerged, discovered a god already here. They asked him where he came from and he said, 'I come from Delyehe, the Seven Stars.' Even the Aztecs believed they originated from the particular constellation that we know as the Pleiades.

When I asked Talks With Bears about this he gave me his own version of the journey of the soul which looked no further than life on earth.

'This is where it is all happening,' he protested. But unlike others who believe one returned again and again to perfect oneself before returning to Great Mystery, he told me, 'Bad people don't get a second chance to come to earth. Only good people come back. Bad people,' he explained, 'have to stand in line for ever and yearn for what they miss. Unlike Christians, we Indians don't believe in heaven or hell. You won't get the Indians thinking about the happy hunting grounds in the sky. For us, the earth is our home. This is where we want to be.'

'And would you want to come back?' I asked.

'Of course,' he said, surprised at my question. 'Don't you?'

'No,' I replied, 'there's too much sorrow on this planet. I wouldn't want to come back.'

He looked at me askance. 'I can't conceive of the idea that anyone wouldn't want to return to the planet.'

He referred to the sweat lodge that Crowhawk would be leading the next day. 'You're in for a treat tomorrow,' he said. 'Crowhawk's a very special, very powerful medicine man and healer. He's descended from Crazy Horse, a notable medicine man of the Sioux, but he's also the most humble, generous man you could meet.'

I asked him how it was that so many half-bloods, like Crowhawk, were teaching the Native ways to white people.

'Half-bloods teach because they know both sides.'

I felt a growing rapport with Talks With Bears and Maka. She was the great-granddaughter of a shaman. Talks With Bears explained that he himself was a mixture of Apache and Irish, with a drop of Spanish thrown in. He was impassioned about living decently and having respect for people's culture and tradition. He had left home at ten and had lived off the streets. In time, he became a heroin addict but had kicked the habit overnight as a young man. 'You can do anything if you just make up your mind to do it.'

His early chequered life gave him an intimacy with down-and-outs, who were later to become the focus of his natural compassion. He began to counsel these outcasts and provided a home for waifs and strays.

'I know where to come when I am feeling lost,' I joked. And, if I thought about it, there was possibly more truth to the statement than I cared to admit. Talks With Bears had a special tolerance for those who kicked over the traces, and a fierce intolerance to prejudice. Mine was definitely an unusual host, and one who was extraordinarily strong-minded.

As we shared a meal together, he continued to chat. 'You know, lots of Irish people came to New Mexico over the years and married Indians. My mother was Irish.' And I had to admit that although he looked Apache, he had a definite Irish gift of the gab.

'The Irish and the Indians have always got on well together,' he confided, 'and in fact Celtic spirituality has a lot in common with ours.'

'Do you mean their nature spirits and their connection to the land?' I queried.

71

'Yes, and lots of little things as well. For example, my mother kept my umbilical cord. Now that's a very Indian thing to do.' He explained that some Indians buried the umbilical cord in a secret place, believing that if it were found by evil spirits they could damage the child.

'Some people even eat the afterbirth,' mused Maka, who had followed the conversation with interest, chipping in with a remark from time to time.

'What did your mother do?' she asked me. There was some hilarity when I confessed that my mother had attempted nothing so adventurous.

'I didn't mean that,' responded Maka, 'I wondered if she had kept it.'

'No, not that either,' I admitted.

I noticed Maka was happy enough for Talks With Bears to do the talking, but she had a lot to add to the conversation when he went out of the room. It wasn't that she was shy about speaking up, but that he was more garrulous than she was.

'Tell us about Pascale,' asked Talks With Bears.

'Well, you'd have loved her. She was vivacious, and kind. Pascale always wanted to adopt orphans. During the troubles in Romania she kept asking if we could take one or two.'

Talks With Bears laughed. 'What were her interests?'

'She loved singing and dancing, but most of her spare time was spent campaigning against cruelty to animals. She was always collecting for some cause or other, and gathering signatures for petitions.'

'How old was she when she died?'

'Fifteen.'

Talks With Bears shook his head and sighed. 'That's a very young age to die, but she must have done everything she came to do.'

'You're right. I've been told many times that she'd learned all she came here to learn, and done all she came here to do. And you know, I believe that. She was beautiful inside and out, and she'd such a wonderful sense of fun.'

Talks With Bears and Maka sat listening, smiling as I described Pascale.

Talks With Bears looked at me with eyes slightly moist. 'I'm honoured to know about Pascale, and to meet you,' he said.

I began to feel an enormous fondness for these two people who could open their hearts and their home to the most needy of strangers. Talks With Bears was remarkably well read, in spite of not being able to read or write until he was a young man. He had strong moral views that had not been handed down to him, but which he had forged himself. I could not help admiring his rough honesty.

By the end of the evening, we had not only exchanged life stories, but had flushed into the open those issues where we disagreed. We were amicable about our different cosmologies. 'It doesn't matter what anyone believes,' said Talks With Bears, 'it is what kind of a human being you are that counts.' On that note we agreed, and decided to call our discussion to a halt.

Maka took me outside to the little casita where I was to sleep. 'Get up when you want,' she said, 'there's no formality here.'

I stayed awake looking up at the stars with a tremendous sense of gratitude. Which of them were the Pleiades? What a beautiful notion it was to believe you came from the stars and returned to them. I remembered one of Pascale's friends telling me that she thought Pascale had become a star. Maybe that was not such a far-fetched idea. The Milky Way was supposedly home to millions of souls in some Native American beliefs.

As I lay in bed thinking of all these things, I let my mind drift back over the events of the day. I was so lucky to have found such people to stay with. Thoughts of the sweat lodge the next day crowded in on me. I was excited about it, but also a bit concerned that it would be too hot, and that I would not be allowed to leave the lodge. Crowhawk had a reputation for being tough on himself and expecting a lot from others. I slept fitfully, in anticipation.

The next morning, Maka was up before me. Talks With Bears came in looking dishevelled with his long hair hanging loose.

'He didn't go to sleep till very late,' explained Maka. 'Come and I'll show you round the place.' She motioned towards the door and we went all around the property. She showed me the site for the sweat lodge and talked about different ideas for improving the landscape. We climbed up on to the rock and sat there chatting about their dream to have a centre where Native wisdom could be taught. 'We could have teepees in the grounds and people could come to stay and learn about different aspects of Native American life.' Maka's eyes shone as she spoke.

I told her I thought it sounded a wonderful idea.

'We want to plant trees to give us more privacy, and make the place a real sanctuary,' she enthused.

'I couldn't imagine a more ideal place to create this,' I told her, 'nor two more perfect people for the task.' I saw a different side to her personality that morning, one that was visionary and decisive. Quick to smile, she was acutely observant, and not easily rattled. I sensed that she did not need attention, but that she could command it when necessary. She had a gentle charm and as many stories and ideas to share as her husband. It was obvious that the two adored each other and I sensed that when things got difficult, her opinion was the one that counted.

Breakfast was a casual affair. Maka said that Crowhawk was expected about eleven as well as her own daughter and son-in-law, but it was after midday before anyone turned up. Talks With Bears' daughter arrived first with her husband. A tall, dark-haired girl with a fair complexion, she had a lively and likeable personality. Her husband, who was Navajo, was shorter and much quieter. He had a strong presence, and features that were reminiscent of a soapstone carving in repose – almond-shaped eyes, a slim nose in a broad face. He seemed very serious but was totally engaging when he smiled.

It was 1.30 p.m. before Crowhawk arrived. 'Indian time' was like 'Eskimo time' and followed a cycle of its own. Things happened when the time was right but not necessarily when arranged. Talks With Bears had supplied the wood for the fire but Crowhawk had offered to bring the rocks. Although there were lots of volcanic rocks which were suitable in New Mexico, one frequently had to travel to get them, and one had to ask permission to take them from the tribe on whose land they were found.

It was 2.30 before we went in to the sweat lodge. I was still uncertain about being part of a ceremony to counteract sorcery, which was a malevolent use of energy, and which carried a weight of its own. I knew that one needed to protect oneself spiritually and psychically when dealing with such negative power, and was worried that I was still too open and vulnerable. My hosts were in a stronger emotional state and I felt they were more in touch with the spirits that would protect them. They were familiar with the spirit world and its idiosyncracies, whereas I was a novice in the field. So I spent a good while making sure I was protected, which I did by invoking the light and imagining myself surrounded by it. Obviously, if anything untoward occurred Crowhawk would deal with it. But the very fact that he had already done several ceremonies, of which this was to be the last, suggested the difficulty of the task he had set himself. Caution and respect were paramount in events such as this, for the safety of all concerned.

Talks With Bears had suggested that I put Pascale's photo on the altar which was set up outside, between the fire and the lodge. Any items people wanted blessed were also put there, alongside the peace pipe and the offerings for the medicine man, which could include tobacco and money, or anything else one wanted to give. I went in after Crowhawk and sat to his right. Maka was to my right, followed by Talks With Bears and their son-in-law. The ground was hard and stony, and I found it difficult to find a comfortable way to sit.

The first round was surprisingly cool, as the rocks seemed to lose their heat rather fast. If the rocks are too porous this can happen and I suspect the ones we used were not as solid as required. I was soon gasping for air, however, as more rocks were put on and I really had to keep a grip on myself not to panic.

'Breathe in the steam,' ordered Crowhawk. 'Think of it as the life-giving breath of Great Spirit.'

I held the thought that the warmth and steam were doing me good but still struggled not to succumb to the intensifying heat.

In the first round, Crowhawk called in the four directions.

Each had its own poetic name and its own particular cosmic archetype, with its own specific function. We were invited to imagine that we visited each direction to receive a message. Crowhawk started with the west. I tried to quieten my racing heart and sensed being given a directive to surrender, to enter the void. From the other directions, I received the words 'protection', 'strength', and 'trust'.

I was calmed by this exercise, and felt I had nothing to fear as regards my safety. But there was still a sense of tremendous relief when we opened the flap. Fresh air gushed in and more coals were added to the pit in the middle. This time we were invited to pray out loud for our personal needs. We took it in turns to voice our deepest hopes and wishes. The effect was remarkable in that it fostered a bonding between all present that would normally have taken years to create. Talks With Bears's words came as a surprise to me.

'Wakan Tanka, I want to welcome Marie to our home and to this lodge. I also want to say how grateful I am to her for bringing a new friend into my life. I am honoured to know about Pascale. She is truly a radiant being. Her love for life and her compassion, which I can see in her eyes, and which inspired her to do so much in her young life so unselfishly for animals and for other people. It humbles me to be in the presence of one with such courage. I ask for blessings upon her, may she always be surrounded by your protection, and return to this earth to inspire others once again.'

It was deeply moving to hear Talks With Bears speak about her in this way, and I found myself crying by the time my own turn came. I asked for the ache in my heart to be healed and for the deeper purpose of her death to be revealed in all the family's lives. As I spoke, the others murmured softly to add their support. When we had all spoken, Crowhawk announced that we would do a healing round for everyone. Each person in turn had to lie head pointing to the fire while the others composed themselves and imagined sending a vortex of healing energy to that person. Meanwhile, the individual to be healed had to imagine that all the negative energy was draining out of the top of the head into the fire.

It was not easy to keep from giving in to the stifling heat, let alone harness one's energy to heal. I felt stretched to the limit on every level, and close to collapse by the time the flap was raised.

'I can't continue,' I thought inwardly. But, as I leaned forward to gasp at the fresh air, I saw the picture of Pascale on the altar. The lower part of her face was masked by several objects, thus enhancing the effect of her beautiful green eyes which looked over at me with their extraordinary clarity and love.

'Keep going, Mum,' I could imagine her saying. I smiled back at the laughing eyes, feeling enormously comforted by her picture.

During the third round, we were told we would have to sit up and give our fullest attention. This was to be a healing round for the sick child and it would need all our effort. The heat of the accumulated rocks felt fierce to me once again, although the others did not seem to be too bothered. Crowhawk led us through a specific and fairly complicated visualization process to protect ourselves and to establish contact with Great Mystery. Once again, we were advised to focus on the breath as a channel for our own healing, and as a vehicle for the healing we were to give the absent child.

It was important that we synchronized our breathing, Crowhawk emphasized, and he began to beat the drum to give us the rhythm. My outbreath was laboured and vocal. I had never had a tolerance for heat of this kind and I was beginning to suffer. Each moment I thought I must give in, I disciplined myself to relax, and imagine that I was breathing in a soothing balm. This staved off the panic, time and time again, and finally got me to the end of the round. Crowhawk thanked each of us for attending the ceremony, explaining that if we had not been there to help he would have had to muster the energy all by himself. Judging by the effort each one of us contributed, that would have been a huge task.

Water was handed round for us to drink and Talks With Bears suggested I pour some over myself to cool off. I was relieved that we had reached the final round, as I think everyone was. In this closing round, Crowhawk drummed and sang with a wild beauty to his voice.

'You'll hear something magical,' Talks With Bears had said, and it was true. Crowhawk had an enchanted voice. He thanked us all again for being there, and I felt a tremendous sense of privilege to have been included. Crowhawk held the pipe reverently in his hands and rolled little balls of tobacco which he pressed into its bowl. It was passed to everybody, and we each sealed our intentions as we puffed its smoke into the air. He finished off by sending it out to the four directions, to above and below and to the centre. It was all done unhurriedly, in a sacred manner.

The air felt cold as we hurried across the yard.

'Marie, you use the shower first,' insisted Maka. I relished the sweet warmth of the water and the good feeling of dry clothes.

We sat together over a meal and they asked about the experiences our family had had of living in north-west Greenland from 1971 to 1973. I had lots of stories to tell, which they seemed to enjoy immensely, and I felt good to be able to contribute in this way. Crowhawk left after a while, and said that he hoped we would see each other again before long, and I thanked him for the privilege of participating in such a special ceremony.

I went to bed deliciously tired after all the energy expended in the lodge. I felt stronger inwardly after the ceremony. The lodge had shown me how one could share one's sweat, and one's breath, in order that another might live. Once again, I had experienced a communion of a kind that is reason alone for attending a purification lodge.

CHAPTER SIX

Feeling At Home

'**I** DON'T WANT TO LEAVE!' THE WORDS BLURTED OUT before I could stop them. Talks With Bears had not yet emerged for breakfast and Maka was sitting by the fireplace puffing a cigarette. We were sipping tea, sharing stories and confidences with the ease of old buddies when the thought of my departure hit me like a cold shower. 'I don't want to go,' I said emphatically.

Maka paused mid-drag and stared at me, her blue eyes wide and enquiring. 'Then stay!' she answered. 'I'll give you some sheets and a duvet, they'll be more comfortable than your sleeping bag.' With that the conversation resumed as if there had been no interruption.

I was stunned at myself. There was something desperate about my desire to stay. I felt an extraordinary kinship with these people and an almost childlike need to be around them and the wholesome and familial qualities that they represented. When Talks With Bears appeared, Maka told him I was staying and he showed no surprise. He looked rather bleary-eyed and sat heavily on one of the chairs.

'I just can't get my energy together today,' he complained. 'I don't know when I've felt so lazy.'

Maka explained that he had just finished a massive building project which had kept him working all the hours of daylight for months.

Maka and I had a walk together after breakfast. Many of the ranches nearby were substantial properties and she complained about the Anglos living on Indian land. This was a sore subject with them and one that preoccupied their thoughts. But a more important issue replaced this concern when the post brought a refusal from the building authorities to accept part of Talks With Bears' plans for a prestigious building in a nearby town.

'They always make things difficult for us people,' complained Talks With Bears. 'And yet Anglos build what they want, even if they're eyesores, and nobody takes a blind bit of notice. They even boast about it. But we can't get permission to build something really beautiful, which would be an asset to the place. It's always the same, they take it out on Hispanics or Indians, but never on Anglos. They get away with murder!' He lapsed into silence for a while, and then added softly, 'I don't want them to take away my creativity. They mustn't take away my creativity.'

This seemed to be the crux of the matter. Talks With Bears could be fiercely independent and courageous when it came to facing authority. But his Achilles' heel was his need for creative freedom, and his refusal to build anything, however utilitarian, that did not enhance the land.

I decided to visit Santa Clara pueblo, and asked Maka if she wanted to join me.

'Another time,' she said conspiratorially. 'I think I ought to stay and try to help Talk With Bears sort this business out.'

I estimated that the journey would take me about a couple of hours. A few miles out of Santa Fe the road opened up to vast red and gold mesas beyond the pinyon-covered hills nearby. The slightly overcast morning cleared to blue skies. I passed two casinos. These have become something of a mixed blessing for the Native Americans, many of whom have them on their land. They bring in a very desirable revenue, but the elders fear that they will destroy family life and other values, and impoverish the spiritual and emotional life of the people. I pulled in at Camel Rock to take a look inside. It was mid-morning and already people were gambling. They were mostly middle-aged and elderly Native Americans. There were a few whites there too. I changed twenty dollars' worth of chips and braved the harsh lights and mind-bending electronic music to look for an empty machine. It took only a few minutes for my money to be gone and a feeling of total energy loss to come over me. I could not wait to get out into the fresh air and sunshine once more.

The contrast between an icon of modern materialism, the casino, and the symbols of a traditional, historic spirituality was brought into relief by my visit to the ancient Puye cliff ruins at Santa Clara. The approach to the ancient site is along a deserted road off the highway. The road began to climb almost immediately through a pinyon-dotted valley to a high plateau at 7,000 feet. The distant Jemez Mountains were clothed in mist. It was desolate. Not a house was in sight. Then suddenly I saw the cliffs, and the signs of dwellings constructed along three terraces of its tawny-coloured face.

Puye was built in the mid-fifteenth century and reached its apogee in 1540. We are told that it was the centre of a Pueblo Indian population that spread out through a number of villages which are still connected by worn trails. 'Pueblo' is a Spanish word for village, but it is also used to describe the type of Indians who live in it. As I gazed up at the cliffs, I noticed that there were two forms of habitation: the caves, and cliff houses which had been built nearby as well as on top of the cliffs. I felt intrigued by the caves, which a fellow traveller said had been used as resonance chambers. I knew that in another part of New Mexico the Tiwa, who are renowned masters of sound, used vibrational effects to 'enhance the psyche' of the community.

I knew from reading Joseph Rael and Elizabeth Marlow's book *Being and Vibration* that 'the Tiwa language is an ancient tongue (not Indian) which was constructed according to different vibratory levels of mother nature'. Language was considered 'an enormous ball of whirling energies which came from the being of goodness'. This power can be harnessed to achieve higher consciousness so that one can commune directly with spirit, and even create miracles. Chanting was not only an act of prayer for the Tiwa people, but was the way of coming into harmony with nature's resonance. Could this have been the same for the Tewa who lived in these cliffs?

Joseph Rael says that 'sound vibration connects the mind,

body, and spirit, and makes the physical body whole. Chanting implants in the psyche the basis for the new and fine-tunes the physical body for both spiritual and mental growth.' Sound chambers had been discovered in an ancient site near Cortez, Colorado. Could some of these chambers in Puye have been used in the same way? I climbed up to the first level and began exploring. Holes of various sizes and shapes were dug out of the cliff face. Some were very small, others were big enough for several people to sit in. There were ruins of brick dwellings alongside these also, but it was the caves which fascinated me. There was no one else around, except for a family picnicking some distance away, so I decided I would try some of the caves out for resonance. But once in them, a sense of awe and mystery descended on me, and I could not bring myself to utter a sound in case I disturbed the ghosts of the past.

I climbed up a steep ladder to the high table-top where I saw more complex and spacious ruins of dwellings around a large ceremonial chamber. The views from the top were magnificent, and the drop to the ground steep. I could see that this would not be an easy place to maraud and, of course, this was one of the reasons why tribes lived in such desolate and inaccessible areas. I began to feel quite breathless after a while but could find no easy way down except back down the ladder. I had not realized how much I had exerted myself climbing up and down the levels, and my legs felt considerably wobbly when I got down.

As I drove back to my new friends, the mountains nearby rose blue and purple beneath the fire-rimmed clouds. Talks With Bears was in a better frame of mind that evening and chatted.

Maka described Talks With Bears' ability to conjure up animals when he was in the wild – one reason she was often reluctant to accompany him on his explorations: 'He often comes face to face with a bear, or deer, or some other wild animal.'

Talks With Bears shifted self-consciously at the kitchen table as she spoke about him.

'It's true, he conjures them up. He feels no fear. He talks to them.'

'Is it true, Talks With Bears?' I asked.

He shrugged, embarrassed. It was no big deal to him.

'And aren't you ever afraid – even of bears?' I asked.

He shook his head. 'They don't want to harm you. There's no wild animal that's purposely out to get you. But if you obstruct them or deliberately get in their way, they'll attack. But only then.'

The subject of meeting animals in the wild brought us to the discussion of vision quests, and my quest in particular. Talks With Bears looked at me very seriously when I told him that I would be expected to fast for three or four days and nights.

'Fasting's a serious thing,' he said emphatically. 'It's not something to be done lightly and you should never do a fast of that duration without first building up to it for at least a year in advance. It's very dangerous to fast if you're unaccustomed to it. The body reacts in strange and unpredictable ways. And especially at your age.' He looked at me rather dubiously. 'Who are these people anyway, who are leading it?'

I told him their names, hoping he would have heard of them but he looked blank. 'They're very well thought of.' I remembered I had said this before recently. 'They've been doing it for years.'

Talks With Bears tapped the table with his finger to emphasize what he was saying 'Believe me, Marie, anybody who expects a middle-aged woman, with no previous experience of it, to be able to fast for four days and nights in the desert doesn't know what they're doing. It's insane and downright irresponsible. Don't do it. Don't do this to yourself, you could seriously damage your health. Don't expect them to be responsible for your safety; you have to be responsible for your own life. Why should you put your life on the line for them?'

I looked at Maka, who indicated that she agreed with him. I was beginning to feel really uncomfortable about the whole situation.

Talks With Bears saw that I was disturbed and he obviously felt guilty. 'Look, don't just take my word for it, and believe me I'm not trying to stop you from doing it. I just want you to know the facts and be able to protect yourself. You know who you should see? You should see Jamie Sams and talk to her. She's an expert on these things, she even leads vision quests herself; and by the way, women's quests are different from men's, they are not as arduous. You shouldn't be doing a man's vision quest in any case. These traditionally were for young men approaching manhood. It was a way for them to test their courage and to ask for a vision for their life mission. Young men need such a challenge,' he said emphatically, 'otherwise they're gonna take drugs or alcohol which satisfies the same urge to prove themselves.'

'Whereas girls, when they reached puberty,' interrupted Maka, 'would go into a moon lodge, which is a bit similar to a sweat lodge, and they would do the equivalent of a vision quest there. Some tribes would have a big celebration to mark her ability to create life, and from then on during her period a woman would go into the moon lodge to relax and ask for vision.'

I felt better when he began to speak of Jamie. She was the very person whom I most wanted to meet. It was Jamie who had devised the Medicine Cards, and the Sacred Path Cards. She was a powerful and well-respected medicine woman, and the inspiration for me to learn about Native American ways in the first place.

'How do I get to meet her?' I asked, impatient to speak to someone who led her own vision quests.

'Well, we had hoped Jamie would've come to the sweat we just did. She lives in Santa Fe and is a good friend of ours. But she's only recently back from a long trip away. I tell you what,' said Talks With Bears. 'One of these days we will ask Jamie over for dinner, and you'll be able to ask her whatever you want.'

I was thrilled and enormously grateful. I did not want to give up the chance of doing my vision quest in California without a proper alternative. But I was beginning to feel strongly that I wanted to do things the woman's way, if I had the choice. I had bought Jamie's latest book, *The Thirteen Original Clan Mothers*, while in Albuquerque, but had not had the chance to read it yet. Its résumé claimed it was: 'Your sacred path to discovering the gifts, talents and abilities of the feminine through the ancient teachings of the sisterhood.' I had barely opened it to see what it was about when my eye caught the phrase 'healing quest'. There in black and white, as if written in answer to my increasing questions, were several pages devoted to explaining why it was that women should do healing quests and not vision quests.

'Women hold their visions inside of themselves in the womb space, and should never be disconnected from the female elements of water and earth,' Jamie had written. The book went on to explain that as women's role is to nurture, receive, and give birth, she must nurture all parts of the self during the healing quest, in order to receive vision and give birth to her dreams. Men, the book explained, require a different approach because they are more outgoing by nature and need the deprivation of food and water to bypass the intellect's hold. She claimed that 'to go beyond limitation, the active male principle must be forced to be still. Through reaching the female side of his nature, the man is then ready to receive his vision.'

I realized that a fundamental shift in the way I participated in life was being introduced to me. I had grown up with six brothers, and had always felt very at home with the masculine psyche and its need to be doing things. The feminine, its familiarity with the dream world, and its connection to the earth had suffered somewhat in my development. I had consciously stopped remembering my dreams in my teens, after an unusually vivid nightmare. And the earth, which children around the world play with for their most creative expression, was not part of my experience as a child. Making mud pies, or even handling the earth, was taboo for us, growing up in Ceylon, as Sri Lanka was then called. The reasons, my father explained, were that there were a number of parasites in the soil that could invade the body through the skin. Thus began a strong alienation from that archetype which helps us ground our dreams and ideas.

'If we are not in good relationship with the earth,' a Native American medicine man told me, 'we get sick and unhappy and wounded in our deepest selves. The only remedy is to get back in touch with Mother Earth. She can heal all wounds.' Only now was I beginning to appreciate how important it was to renew my connection to this source.

At breakfast the next day I told Maka that I was thinking of going to Jemez that morning.

'Oh, but we've a very special place that we want you to see, and we thought we'd go there today,' she explained.

Talks With Bears seemed preoccupied over breakfast but afterwards he came over to me with his hand outstretched. 'Take a look at this.'

I saw a minute mother of pearl shell in the palm of his hand, with a hole through it to suggest that it had been part of a necklace.

'This is ancient,' he said solemnly. 'It's sacred too. I found it at the place we're going to see today the last time I was there. I thought when I saw it, I'd like to give that to my granddaughter. But, you know, there's some unhappy spirit there because of it. When I left, I felt a hand grab me on the shoulder, like that.' He placed a heavy grip on my shoulder as he looked worriedly at me. 'You know, nothing has gone right since I took this. So I'm going to take it back today.'

Maka looked at me pointedly and shrugged. 'He's convinced all this has to do with him taking that itsy-bitsy piece of shell.'

'Well, I'm going to take it back, anyway,' Talks With Bears said defiantly. 'What do you think?' He looked hard at me.

'I think you should, if you feel that way about it,' I answered, 'but I can't believe the spirits would mind you taking it, especially for your granddaughter.'

I noticed ominous black clouds appearing on the horizon. 'It looks as if it's going to rain,' I commented.

'No, no; it won't rain here,' said Talks With Bears.

I didn't like to contradict him, since he lived in the place and was almost a nature spirit himself, but I decided I would take my rain gear in any case.

'Maka, where's the tobacco?' Talks With Bears fussed around the mantelpiece as he asked her. 'I want to make a tobacco tie.'

Maka waved towards the other side of the mantelpiece and Talks With Bears rooted among things to the side of its little altar for some thread. He was totally engrossed as he made a little pouch from a square of red material which he filled with tobacco and tied. There was something almost childlike about the reverence with which he threaded the tiny piece of shell to it. He looked at me with a glance that showed it was a task well done, and pocketed it. I was still making sandwiches and Maka was testing her rucksack to make sure it was not too heavy when he called to us to look outside.

'See, there's a hawk. It's a sign. I'm going to get a message.'

We had to drive a good way before parking the van near a dry riverbed. We must have walked along it for half an hour or more then headed off through the bush. The ground began ro rise, and as we walked along, Talks With Bears pointed out various rocky outcrops where he said there were wonderful pictographs. They were steep and shaly, and he advised me not to climb them, since it would take up too much time and would be rather hazardous.

'If people knew they were here they would steal them. That is why we don't let many people know about the place.'

I had felt a few rather fat drops on my nose and could see the black clouds gaining on us. 'Here comes the rain.' I watched as what looked like a solid wall advanced across the valley towards us. I hurriedly donned my waterproofs.

We trudged on for an indeterminate while, getting wetter and wetter, until I heard a call from Maka.

'This is it!' She was excited, and began to cast among the rubble of moss-covered stones for pottery shards. 'There's lots of them,' she called.

Talks With Bears picked up a couple of pieces and handed them to me. I looked at the grey pieces which were patterned with black. 'Those are ancient,' he said, and pointed to some I had not seen near my feet.

It took me a while to distinguish them between the earth and stones, but then I kept seeing them everywhere. The site was not large, only a few clusters of dwellings that had long since been empty. My companions surveyed it affectionately.

'Isn't it wonderful?' asked Maka.

I nodded, speechless.

Maka found refuge under the branches of one of the trees near the summit and lit a cigarette. 'See, there is where the women used to grind the corn,' she said, pointing to an indented stone nearby.

'Who did you say lived here?'

'Probably the Anasazi, or their descendants. It must have been round about the time of Christ. I don't know really. We don't want to draw attention to the site by asking or people would come and take everything away.'

It was obvious that these were a people who liked living together in community. They were the forefathers of the Pueblo Indians who, to this day, live in close community with each other. Their neighbours, the Navajos, were not so gregarious.

Talks With Bears began walking away purposefully, wrapped in his own thoughts. I wondered if anyone else might find his little offering with the small shell attached to it in the future. What story might they make of it? The rain filtered through the branches on to Maka and me as we sat there, and I found myself trying to imagine what life must have been like on this remote hill-top.

'Isn't it just the most amazing place?' enthused Maka.

'It really is,' I agreed. 'I'm so grateful that you brought me here.'

After a while, she suggested that we go and find Talks With Bears. I replaced the pottery shards on the ground. Talks With Bears had already explained that we should take nothing so as to respect the history and the specialness of the place. It was a good feeling to be able to enjoy something which one regarded as treasure, and yet not take it away. I was so used to collecting little bits of memorabilia from the different places I visited. This was the first time I had found something remarkable and enjoyed it for its own sake without indulging the desire to possess it. It was an empowering thing to do.

Talks With Bears led off with the two of us following. We splashed through streams and around and over rocks to where Talks With Bears said there was a special cave. The entrance to it was camouflaged by further rocks, but the blackened roof showed that once it had been home to many fires. Talks With Bears looked around with an obvious reverence.

'I left some tobacco ties here,' he said, becoming quite anxious when he could not see them.

'They're up on that bit of a ledge in front of the blow hole,' comforted Maka.

He felt up for them and seemed satisfied that no stranger had been in the cave since his last visit.

I asked if there was a special reason for making the ties.

'No. It's just out of respect. I wanted to thank the cave for letting me visit it, and to apologize if I had disturbed any of the spirits.' He looked around. 'I don't tell many people about this place.'

I felt particularly privileged, not only to have been invited to see it, but because I was sharing an intimate moment with my host. This respect and love for nature was so much a part of the Native American way. The idea that we give back something to nature if we take from her was created from a consciousness that lived in harmony with its environment.

Talks With Bears pointed to the roof of the cave which was furred with a thick layer of soot in several places. 'They must've had three fires going at times. Two or three families could've sheltered in here.' He sat on the natural seat created by the floor of the biggest section of the cave, which was about four feet off the ground, and let his gaze roam. 'Those are very ancient fireplaces,' he said with awe. It was evident that the cave held a unique place in his heart: it was a tangible link to a time when the ancestors, the ancient ones, the keepers of the wisdom of the nations walked the land.

On the way home, Maka talked about some of the homes she and Talks With Bears had built. Building was a sacred art to both of them. She wanted to build a hogan in the back yard and said how they would lay turquoise at the base of each post to protect it, and keep its intention pure. This, she explained, was a way of dedicating it. She told me that Navajos always hold a purification and dedication ceremony before living in a place, to ward off evil spirits.

We were soaked through by the time we arrived home. Maka joked that she wished she'd listened to me and taken some waterproof clothing, but in fact I was almost as damp as they were. We cooked a meal together and sat chatting into the night about the difference between white people and Navajos, one of which, said Talks With Bears, was that the Navajos were always curious about who you are, where you come from and who were your family and ancestors. I remembered Marina explaining that by introducing yourself according to the clans of her grandparents, her relatives would acknowledge her and help her in need.

'White people always want to know what you do. They judge you by sight, whether you are rich, or have a good job, or have good looks. I don't judge beauty by the appearance of somebody, I judge beauty by how they are, what kind of a human being they are,' said Talks With Bears. He went on to talk about one of his relatives by his daughter's marriage, who was the only person to survive the removal of the tribe from their homelands to Fort Sumner. The present clan originates from this great-grand-mother. She survived for years on her own, while her people were suffering in prison. She lived in the mountains and did not come down until her people returned. It was an awesome thought to imagine this woman on her own in those dangerous times and all the clanspeople who owed their lives to her courage. I was beginning to dream more and, that night, my dreams were inspired by stories of the Navajos and the sounds of the coyotes barking in the nearby fields.

CHAPTER SEVEN

Feast Day

SATURDAY, 12 NOVEMBER, THE DAY OF MY DEPARTURE, dawned grey and drizzling. At Talks with Bears' suggestion, I made a little altar in the car as protection, and as a tribute to Pascale.

'Make an altar wherever you go,' he urged. 'Some little things from nature will do it for it, or something that's special for you, a picture of Pascale for example, some sage or cedar, and a crystal maybe, or even a feather.'

I had, in fact, carried a beautiful photo of Pascale, and another of the family, which I placed on the seat beside me. They gave me a sense of connectedness.

Talks with Bears also told me that when the Native Americans want to contact someone who has died, they make a medicine pouch and put something inside that belongs to that person. 'Make one for yourself,' he suggested, 'and let it hang close to your heart and when you feel upset, just hold it to your heart and breathe through it.'

I said I would.

'Where'll you go?' Maka asked.

'I don't know yet. Maybe to Jemez. They're having a feast-day today.'

'Be careful of the snow on those mountains,' warned Maka.

I knew my car would not perform well in snow but I wanted to take a chance on it. As I left the driveway, I turned towards Santa Fe. The least I could do would be to drive in the direction of Jemez and then if the weather got too bad, I would stop somewhere and maybe come back.

I drove north out of Santa Fe and made good time to San Idelfonso reservation. I had been tempted by a beautiful patch of blue sky, which appeared through the dark clouds with the promise of fairer weather. But as I started to climb through great canyons, I discovered that the promise had been false. The landscape gave way to green-grey spectre-like rocks which were not at all cheery. Soon I was surrounded by mist and rain. The road climbed steeply and tortuously through and around the mountains. Sometimes the hazard was to one side with a sheer drop into the mist, at other times the threat was from landslides or rocks bouncing off the escarpment. The road signs warned of these, but I had no idea some of them could be as large as boulders until I came across several of them on the road and just managed to zigzag around them.

I had to go through Los Alamos, the place where the nuclear bomb was developed. The mist obscured much of the town but could not disguise the fact that it was set among dense forests. I stopped to ask directions of a smartly dressed man coming out of a government building.

'I wouldn't go into the mountains unless you have to,' he warned. 'There was a lot of snow yesterday and more is forecast later.'

I grimaced as I wound up the window. I was tempted to take a chance on getting through, but I did not want to get stuck. As long as I could get back to Los Alamos in an emergency, I would be all right.

I was conscious of how deserted was the green alpine wilderness as I drove on. The road began to rise again rapidly and I had to slow to a snail's pace to negotiate the narrow hairpin bends with their steep drop on the nearside. Snow still carpeted the ground, but it had turned to slush on the road. That, together with the frequent rock slides, made driving a slow and hazardous experience. I was nervous and tense, as much from the isolation as the conditions of the road. Any cars I saw were all going in the opposite direction. What did they know that I did not?

There are occasions when time moves agonizingly slowly, second by second. Each moment seems an eternity when you are labouring up a mountain. And that split second when you realize that you have at last crested the rise and the nose of the car is pointed downhill, becomes a moment of immense joy and relief. I could hardly believe I had got through the Jemez Mountains but, as I descended their other side, the land opened up to meadows, and to the occasional farm or mountain home. The rain stopped and I entered the valley into Jemez Springs to see lots of aspen still in leaf. Hardier folks than myself had braved the steep muddy slopes to natural hot springs tucked away in the woods. I could hear their voices through the trees when I parked the car.

The Jemez Valley is flanked by hugh towering rock ridges. Supporting a high mesa, they protected the Jemez Indians from both missionaries and soldiers. And when finally it was safe enough to build their pueblo in the valley, they found it lush and nurturing and beautiful. I stopped at one of the inns for a late breakfast and enquired about the festival at the Pueblo.

'It's on all day,' responded the proprietor, and she asked if I would like company, as she intended to go for a couple of hours herself. I was delighted at the offer, and we left after I had eaten.

We drove through a valley with towering red rocks on one side and beautiful high mountains on the other. The river was in spate and in several places streams ran blood red across the road. I was reminded of our home in Devon where we had the same coloured soil. After about fifteen minutes' drive, the valley opened out and I saw a large pueblo, clustered with adobe houses, from where I could hear drumming and singing.

We parked on the road to the village, which had become a sea of mud. We squelched through it up to our ankles, taking care not to step out of our boots which at times stuck fast. Down two lanes there were booths, with visitors from other pueblos selling their wares, the ubiquitous silver and turquoise. The boom of the drum pulled us to the large plaza where several hundred people, Indians and Anglos, stood in the rain to celebrate the pueblo's feast.

We stood in the mud, slipped in the mud, and at least 600 men, women and children that day danced in the mud! The repetitive drum beat was accompanied by deep male voices. The male dancers wore a tunic from the waist down, with an ornamental sash which hugged the waist and hung down one side. Their chests were bare but painted blue, with a string of fluted shells across the chest and shoulder. Bells hung from the belt and a fox skin hung down the back. They wore white moccasins on their feet and their heads were sometimes adorned with a topknot and feathers.

The women had embroidered dark tunics from neck to knee, worn over white blouses. Their headdresses stood about twelve inches high and were wooden, with different fretwork designs. There was a unity and presence about the dancers which was deeply moving. Rather than cowering from the elements, they accepted them as though they were an integral part of the ceremony. There was a mindfulness about them that gave them dignity, in spite of the ravages of the rain and mud.

To the right, the flash of red-gold hair amongst raven locks caught my attention. I saw a fair-skinned girl of about fifteen dancing amid a large group of the village youngsters. She stood out because of her fairness, as well as her obvious sense of fun, but, other than that, she was at one with the rest of her peers who seemed to enjoy the camaraderie of the event. Watching them brought a lump to my throat and a strange wistfulness. I felt my eyes moisten as I watched her carefree smile and the sense of kinship with which she accompanied the villagers in the simple but repetitive dance. The mud curled over their beautiful white moccasins but this only added to the enthusiasm with which they continued the dance. I knew another fifteen-year-old who had laughed that same delightful way, and I felt myself flooded with a host of memories, associations and wishful thinking. I could just imagine Pascale entering into the spirit of such an occasion.

When the first group had finished dancing, a second lot, of about 200 people who had been waiting by the side, stepped forward. I was amazed at their good humour while standing around in the rain. The men especially must have felt cold, for this group were also bare-chested, painted with a brown dye this time. Good humour was definitely the order of the day. The dances between one group and another did not seem to differ that much. And even within the dance, the steps were minimal and repetitive, changing slightly with the rhythm of the drum. I was struck by the tremendous sense of community exhibited by the dancers. Old people and young children took part, all dressed virtually the same, except for a few clownlike characters in masks who rode among the crowd on hobby horses.

Chilled vendors huddled under blankets in the different stalls. It had been a long vigil, since early morning, for them. Although the dances were still continuing, spectators had begun to drift away. We were soaked to the skin by the time my companion and I returned to the inn.

I dried out before going for a mineral bath in the spa, where I luxuriated in the warm water.

That evening I sat chatting with the proprietor of the inn over my meal. She talked about Jemez and its strange capacity to stir up people's moods. She explained that there was something about the energy of the village that disrupts people's lives before it can heal them. It was a place of strong women, where men often feel threatened and leave. The very fact that there are so many different religious groups in the village suggested that they had all tapped in to some rarefied spiritual essence.

But alongside all the lightness and spirituality there was a darker side. 'It is a place where you get heartbreak and betrayal,' confided one of the locals to me, but would not be drawn to explain herself. Maybe it was this power that caused such disruption. There are some places which act like a purge on one's emotions and it seemed Jemez was such a place.

I had experienced it myself without realizing that Jemez could have triggered it. For, on returning from the pueblo, I had felt suddenly deeply leaden-hearted. I began to miss the family dreadfully and was overwhelmed with a sense of aching loss. When I put out the picture of Pascale by my bedside I burst into uncontrollable weeping. I could not sleep that night and felt burdened with grief. How long did one mourn the death of a child? I asked myself. It seemed as if I had endless layers of heartache to offload. I gazed at Pascale's picture. It always comforted me, although now I wept at the finality of her absence. We seek the beloved in form, or aim to capture the beloved in form that we can take hold of – but the beloved is beyond form. Where did those words come from into my mind? I didn't find them at all comforting. I understood so much about grief, and about letting go, but that did not stop me hurting.

A huge tear landed on my tape recorder and immediately I had a mental image of myself at home one day, soon after Pascale had died, discovering a revision tape of hers on which she had read her German vocabulary out loud. I struggled with myself for ages, wanting to put it on just to hear her voice, even if it was only homework. I stopped myself from listening to it and got rid of the tape. I was so conscientious during those forty days' challenge. I was so tempted to hang on to things that would remind me of her physically, while at the same time trying to let her go. But it did help if I made an effort to transform my pain into love that I could constantly beam at her from my heart.

Each of us in the family had to deal with things at their own pace. Wally or Kari might need the physical comfort of certain of her things longer than me. What is right for one is not necessarily right for another. I was pushing for transcendance of the process as quickly as possible, not only to avoid hindering Pascale's continuing soul journey, but because I knew the prize of going through the pain barrier, and dealing with grief, is communion at a golden level. My will might push me to transcend my feelings but my feelings would have their say, and the atmosphere of Jemez seemed to collaborate with any unexpressed emotion. 'Nobody hugs like you, Pascale,' I said out loud. And I really missed this physical and emotional sustenance. I wrote in my diary, 'I ache deep inside.'

If I thought about things, I had come a long way. In the early days of Pascale's going, I had thought that the breakdown of our routine and the disruption of our plans would last forever. I seemed to have a lot of spare time with nothing to do in it. All sense of commitment and responsibility and purpose had vanished. What is the point of being alive? I had asked. What is the point of my life? I would have to reorder my life . . . we all would. This journey showed that I had the ability to commit to something. I was willing to find new purpose in my life.

The next morning I wanted to move off early back to Gallup but breakfast was not until nine, so I had to delay. The sky looked radiantly blue but there were dark clouds forming. The road had dried but I did not realize how sodden the earth was until I got stuck in it when getting out of the car to take a picture. My feet sank into the ground before I was aware of its loose consistency, and they looked like mud boats when I pulled them out. I might as well get my picture while I was at it, I thought, but I would have been better not to have left the car.

I was caked to the knees by the time I could sit back in the vehicle and I had a difficult job to remove my filthy shoes and find another pair. People from a passing car hooted at me when they saw me looking so stricken, but they did not stop to offer help. All in all, I was feeling pretty miserable and fed up, and only barely managed to back the car out of the sludge after a great deal of care and patience. Jemez had still not finished working its potency on me and I found myself agonizing about the loss of Pascale once again, tormented by the sense of finality.

When I arrived in Gallup back at Jenni's where I had spent those first few days in New Mexico, I found it was her birthday. She was in the middle of cooking a lovely meal, and seemed very glad to see me, while showing alarm to find I was so breathless.

'Are you OK? You're puffing an awful lot.'

I had not thought about it, but these days I seemed to get breathless with the slightest exertion. I had put it down to the altitude, which was about 6,500 feet, but Jenni said I should get it checked out.

The next day I decided to visit the shops at the other end of town, and discovered a quaint old-fashioned establishment in a side street which declared on a notice that it mended and made jewellery. There was a buffalo skull in the window and some interesting Native American artefacts. Inside, it was a treasure trove, with all sorts of oddments, bric-à-brac, and cases full of jewellery. Feathers of all kinds hung from the wall alongside leather pouches, dream catchers, pipes and shields. I got chatting with the jeweller, a white man, who was poring over some intricate jewellery work on his desk.

After a while, a young Navajo woman came in and asked to see his leather scraps. I saw her choosing several pieces from the bundle and could not refrain from asking her what she was going to do with them.

'Make Katchina dolls,' she answered sweetly, and at that the jeweller interrupted.

'That's what you should do. You should go to the Shalako Dances at Zuni Pueblo on 3 and 4 December, and see the Katchinas. They're huge masked figures that impersonate the gods. They're well worth seeing because after a while they actually become possessed by the gods.'

On the way home, I bought a feather fan and some cedar which I could use to smudge myself with.

'Are you a medicine woman?' the assistant asked me. She was about my age and a Native American.

'No, but I'm a therapist.'

'Then you should have a rattle.' She picked several up and tested each sound against her ear. 'This would be good for you,' she said. 'It has a feminine sound.'

The rattle, like the fan, had been beautifully made. It consisted of a small gourd attached to a beaded handle, and had a leather fringe hanging from the base. On top of the gourd was a bead to which was attached a tuft of horsehair. Drums and rattles are used frequently in much Native American ceremonial. They can induce a near trance state, and at other times can summon a person back from their inner journeying.

Grandmother Spider had once explained the drum as representing 'the heartbeat of Mother Earth. Just as the child in the womb is comforted by the mother's heartbeat, so if we tune in to Mother Earth we will be comforted by her heartbeat. The earliest drums were from hollow logs which were covered with hides. People beat on them with whatever came to hand, often a leftover animal bone.' Today, the drum is used in ritual to connect people with a different state of consciousness. You can journey with the drumbeat to other realities while feeling anchored and protected by its resonance.

The rattle serves as an aid in much the same way. It can break up negative energy in the aura and summon the helping spirits. The shaking of a rattle is said to be the symbolic movement of life forces.

The next day an insurance form arrived for the vision quest in the Californian desert. A medical was asked for and comprehensive insurance to cover the possibility of all sorts of emergency treatment.

'Your blood tests show that you have a hyperthyroid condition,' the doctor carrying out my medical told me. 'In the circumstances, I would advise against you fasting on your vision quest.'

I heard the news with some dismay. This might explain my fatigue, restlessness and insomnia but how would it affect my ability to do the quest?

Zuni Pueblo, where the Shalako Dances were to take place, is south of Gallup, and about five to six hours' drive from Santa Fe where I had been staying. I had been told they were not to be missed but that only the second part of the ceremony was open to visitors, the first part being only for the initiated. I left Santa Fe at about 10.00 a.m. to arrive in good light so that I could find my way about. I had no real idea what to expect other than that the festivities lasted all night. 'The dances are different from anything you'll experience anywhere else,' I had been told. 'In these dances, it is the spirits themselves who take part. They're known as Katchinas, and they're generally benevolent.'

The Zuni believed they owed everything to the Katchinas, who had taught their ancestors how to farm, dance, hunt, weave, and even to make pottery, jewellery and baskets. When the people needed rain, the gods would dance in the fields and rain would come. If the people were miserable, the gods would dance for them, and bring them happiness and joy. But the good times had not lasted and evil came. The people and the spirits fought and the spirits fled and refused to return.

Naturally, if the spirits that govern your lives vanish, so does your prosperity, and once that has gone, there is nothing much left to enjoy. In despair the people went to the gods and pleaded with them to return, but the gods were adamant in their refusal until, in time, they agreed to a compromise. The people could impersonate them and do the rituals and ceremonies. The men dressed themselves in wigs and masks, feathers and claws, and danced so well that the gods decided to reward them. In future when they danced, the gods would enter and possess them. The gods themselves would dance.

The Zuni, like other tribes, have a religion which is integrated into every aspect of life. Dhyani Ywahoo, a Cherokee spiritual teacher, says that 'Native religion is a whole way of life, based on everything being in relationship. The sacred rituals are to maintain harmonious balance of the energy currents of the sun, moon, earth, and the entire universe, so that the seed's bounty can be brought forth.' The Shalako Dances, in which the Katchinas take part, are exactly for this reason, to promote wellbeing among the community and to make the earth fecund, and the crops and animals plentiful. I wanted to experience the vitality of such ceremonies.

I had been on the road for over three hours when I saw a sign to Zuni that promised a picturesque route. With seventy-five miles still to go, I welcomed the more intimate drive through villages and countryside that small roads afford. The road linked Hispanic villages with outlying ranches through wild desolate areas, and on through forest and mesa, pinyon grove and sandstone cliffs. I passed a sign to the Perpetual Ice Caves, another of New Mexico's strange anomalies of nature, and marvelled that extinct volcanoes and ice caves could share the same space.

It was a lonely but beautiful drive, and I was glad when I finally reached Zuni in the late afternoon. I looked for a performance space, such as a square or large arena, and was firmly put in my place when I enquired about the performance.

'There's no performance,' the young woman I had stopped to ask directions told me. 'The Katchinas don't perform. They dance in sacred ceremony.'

I felt a bit put out. I didn't like to intrude on people's sacred ceremony, and I had been led to believe that there were dances one could attend.

'You can watch the dances,' the woman said, 'but they won't start dancing until 1.00 a.m. You can get a map of the village and the ceremonial houses where the Katchinas will dance in any of the shops.'

I drove further until I came to what seemed to be the hub of the old part of the town. The houses were traditional flat-roofed stone or adobe dwellings. I noticed that a lot of dogs ran loose, some of them friendly, but others threatening. I parked the car and strolled past the knot of people loitering near clay ovens where bread was being baked for the evening feasts. People chatted animatedly while children darted around squealing and shrieking between yapping dogs. I overheard someone telling a visitor that although the ceremony had already started on the other side of the river, an area forbidden to outsiders, we could all watch the participants processing through the streets around 7.00 p.m. The Katchinas would go to one or other of several ceremonial houses where they would remain till midnight, praying and blessing the place.

After an hour's rest, the Katchinas would start dancing, and one could watch the proceedings through the windows of the houses. We were obviously in for a long wait.

The night was memorable for the hours of anticipation that kept me, and many others, moving from one ceremonial house to another for we knew not what. The build-up to the ceremony, with its air of secrecy and taboo, had acted like a stimulant to the visitors' mood. People drifted from place to place, chatting and laughing as they negotiated various objects in the dark. It contrasted with the reverential demeanour of the locals taking part in one of the ceremonies in the Long Horn ceremonial house. The interior of the rectangular room was bedecked with gorgeous shawls, rugs, jewellery and other personal items that people wanted blessed, and which hung on the walls between the mounted heads of deer. The room was crowded with men, women and children. The men participating in the ceremony wore white with various accoutrements giving a splash of colour.

The Zuni are famous for their complex ritual ceremonies which to an outsider might seem repetitive, long-winded and static. Around each window of the Long Horn House, sightseers thronged, staring in. I felt uncomfortable in the role of voyeur. This was not a spectacle to be gawped at, but a sacred ceremony with deep significance for the local people. I imagined how I would feel if I were at a similar ceremony and found myself being scrutinized by tourists.

'The Katchinas do not come to this place,' an American woman in her sixties explained to me. 'This is the Long Horn House, a totally different ceremony. If you want to see Katchinas, you should go to some of the other houses.'

'But I don't like to intrude,' I said.

'You won't if you're respectful like you seem to be.'

Bonfires had been lit near the ceremonial houses, a necessity rather than a luxury, as it would have been intolerably cold to hang around in the open for so many hours without their heat to cheer and warm one. They were great places to meet and chat with people, and I was amused to talk to a young Navajo lad who knew as little about the procedure as I did.

'I was shocked to find there was no place for people to perform,' he told me. 'I didn't know I'd have to walk miles in the dark. I'm freezing,' he admitted as he hunched over the fire. He was dressed in a thin shirt and jumper, with no jacket.

'It's going to be a long night,' I joked.

He laughed, as did several others. And some friendly banter was exchanged between everyone. There were several Navajo men around the fire who admitted that they had not known what to expect either.

'I like to come and see other people's ceremonies,' a man next to me of about forty, dressed in Western clothes, with long hair pulled back in a ponytail, said, 'but we Navajo have a lot of powerful ceremonies of our own.'

At long last, I heard the sounds of chanting carried through the night air from some distance down the road. Lights bobbed up and down in the darkness, marking the progress of the procession along the dark country road. After a while a group of men, dressed in white ceremonial garb with a ribbon tied around their foreheads, came marching alongside an exotic giant figure.

'That's the Katchina,' one of the Navajo men whispered to me.

As it approached, a group of women rushed forward to greet it. I could not see whether they had touched it or showered something over it. As it neared the door of the building, an elaborate blessing ceremony began.

'They're spreading cornmeal about. It's like an offering,' one of the men explained.

I joined the gang of onlookers at the window to watch proceedings.

A second elaborate blessing ceremony took place inside the entrance and lots of ritual gestures were made to the different directions. Two of the celebrants performed their duties with a clutch of feathers which they used to fan the air in a circular motion. They were dressed in a kilt-like tunic under a maroon velvet jacket. They wore moccasins on their feet and a string of bells around their ankles. Their white hats looked like upturned flowers with the stalk protruding. The appearance of these celebrants heightened the intensity. Then the eyes of all were turned on the giant figure of the Katchina as it progressed to the end of the long hall where, behind a screen formed by the other celebrants, the top part of the body, which included the mask, was removed from its wearer and placed on a cushion facing the congregation.

I had the impression that the figure was still alive, even if stationary. In the hours that followed, the lengthy emergence myth was recounted. As that was going on, people sat at a table in the balcony room adjacent, eating. Where there is no separation between the sacred and the profane, every aspect of life is considered sacred. I watched for an hour or more before returning to the fire. The easy camaraderie that had begun earlier continued. People exchanged stories and gossip.

As we were talking, waves of laughter bore down on us from a crowd surrounding a group of men dressed in white. Every time one of these spoke in Zuni, the crowd howled with laughter.

'Who are they?' I asked.

'They're a bit like clowns,' a young, well-built Zuni youth answered.

'What are they saying?' I asked.

He screwed his face up, looking for the right words. 'It's difficult to translate; it's about . . . sex.'

I laughed. There was hardly a more difficult subject to translate.

He listened to the banter of the people around the fire and then introduced himself. 'I'm Thomas.'

'And I'm Marie. Are you Zuni?'

He filled his chest out before responding, 'You bet, one hundred per cent. I'm a full-blood.'

I was touched by the pride in his voice.

By midnight, there was an air of anticipation as people began to crowd around the windows to catch a glimpse of the Katchinas dancing. But it was 1.00 a.m. before the spectacle began. Drums and rattles accompanied the chanting as the mythical being processed along the length of the hall with its simple two-step. The monotonous rhythm dulled the senses which the cold and tedium of waiting had numbed. My legs ached with standing but there was something which impelled one to move from window to window, and house to house, for that elusive glimpse of the gods dancing.

The further into the night, the colder it got. By five in the morning, I had had enough and got into the car exhausted. Zuni boasted no hotel so it was seven a.m. before I crawled into Grants, a small country town off the motorway, and pulled into the first available motel. I hardly had time to take off my boots before my eyelids shut out the world. For once insomnia released its grip and sleep was never so sweet.

CHAPTER EIGHT

Women's
Medicine

THE LAND OF ENCHANTMENT IS HOW NEW MEXICANS describe their high-altitude state. Desert, mesa and mountain have bred a stock of hardy indigenous people, Pueblo Indians in the main, whose battle to survive culturally against the Spaniards in the sixteenth century was often more difficult than any natural hardship. Today, a small part of the Navajo nation extends into New Mexico from Arizona, and a group of Mescalero Apaches also make this state their home. Besides these, the Pueblo Indians share their homeland, for the most part, with Hispanics and Anglo-Americans.

A chance meeting in a gallery was how I met my host, Karen, when I visited Santa Fe the first time. I had long heard that Santa Fe was one of the art capitals of the world and that no visit was complete without seeing some of the fabulous south-western and Indian art in its many exhibitions and galleries. It was Maka who made me realize that the art was as inseparable as spirituality in their culture and their life, and was often connected to the spiritual. 'You've got to see some of the Native sculpture,' Maka told me. 'Indian art can take its place anywhere in the world.'

I had feasted my soul on many of these treasures and was about to leave the city when I was drawn to look at one last gallery.

Once inside the door, I stopped in my tracks, mesmerized by three large alabaster sculptures. 'My, those are beautiful!' I exclaimed and stood gazing at them for some time. I was aware of someone sitting behind the desk but had not looked to greet her, so taken was I by the figures.

'They're pretty wonderful,' came the soft-spoken reply and I turned to see a smiling, tall, silver-haired woman. As our eyes met, I knew I liked her. There was an openness to her expression and friendliness that was engaging. 'The artist has just been in,' she continued. 'What a pity you missed him.'

I was torn between wanting to talk to her and looking at all the fascinating things she had in the gallery. My new friend, for friend she was to become, sensed this and let me wander and gaze. I was conscious of her presence hovering like some benevolent being. When the moment was right, she pointed out special objects, and told me stories about them or the artists who had made them. I was taken by a life-size cradle board and doll. It had been beautifully fashioned, and hanging from it were a small rattle, and a miniature medicine pouch. Painted on the curved bar over the head was a star.

'That's the child's medicine symbol. It represents the essence of the baby. Cradle boards such as this were often buried after the child had grown out of it, in order to protect symbolically the essence of the child from any being or entity that might want to harm it. Some tribes used to hang the cradle boards from the boughs of trees when the mothers were working in the fields, hence the lullaby, "Hush-a-bye baby on the tree top".'

I looked at my informant with surprise.

She laughed. 'That was an Indian lullaby until the pilgrims adopted it.'

'What are you doing in Santa Fe?' she asked.

Once again, I explained about the quest which had brought me here, and my hopes of meeting medicine people.

'Well, if you ever need a room, I've got one spare,' she offered. 'Here, I'll give you a business card and put my home number on it. Don't hesitate to call me any time.'

And so it was that I came to be staying in Santa Fe with Karen, who offered me her home as a base for as long as I needed it. I marvelled at the way things were working out for me, but I wasn't the first stranger Karen had taken under her roof. Like Talks with

Bears and Maka, Karen too attracted people to her who needed a helping hand, and she loved the companionship and new horizons that this brought her.

Santa Fe is at an altitude of nearly 7,000 feet and is the oldest capital within the boundaries of the United States. It has been called an 'energy centre' and gives sanctuary to all manner of spiritual disciplines and alternative lifestyles.

I was curious to meet Dr Vivian King who had trained in psychosynthesis, the form of transpersonal psychology that I had studied, because of her interest and work on the 'Inner Theatre'. Using the model of the theatre with its playwright, director, players and play, she had created a lively model for personal growth work, which I wanted to discuss with her. An attractive and vibrant lady in her forties, she exuded confidence and competence. I visited her home not far out of Santa Fe, in the pinyon-covered hills, and chatted about colleagues we both knew and about what was happening in our lives at the moment. When I told Vivian about my quest, she made a comment which brought a painful clarity to me: 'It's time for you to disidentify from the role of mother.'

For a moment I felt as if I had been doused with a cold shower. I am a mother so how could I disidentify from that? And then the wisdom of what she had said reminded me of what I had learned in my own training, but which for the moment I had forgotten: my selfhood was infinitely larger and more versatile than my strong identification with motherhood might allow me to experience. If we identify with motherhood to the exclusion of the rest of our gifts and talents, then we are devastated when our children leave home. I had enjoyed a career as a writer and part-time therapist at the same time as I had enjoyed motherhood, but I realized in this instant that although I was willing to release Pascale, I had not even thought about releasing my attachment to mothering.

Maybe that was why I had been drawn intuitively to search for the feminine. I was searching for the larger part of myself which exists beyond but which includes the role of being a mother. Just seeing this was sufficient for me to tap into that larger context of the process happening to me. I felt grateful to Vivian for voicing this insight, even though at first I had not wanted to hear it. The irony was that I had helped other people to acknowledge this and to look at their lives differently and I now had to do it for myself. One of the most powerful learnings during my training was the concept that each of us is a crowd. At any one moment, one or other of the different aspects of our psyche may be pulling our strings, deciding our fate or experience. How else is it possible that we can espouse two totally opposite and contradictory views at any given moment, or that we can love someone and hate them at the same time?

The reason is that we are multi-faceted, multi-dimensional beings with a numinous self which infuses a personality. When we are 'centred' we identify with and express the qualities of the self, but too often we allow ourselves to be pulled off centre into one or other of the host of 'characters' that make up our personality. The result is a warped view of ourselves, of life and of our role in it. We can identify with parenthood, with our job, with being male or female, a teacher, student, or any other role that we play in life. We can even identify with an emotion, sadness, anger, or being a victim. Whatever we identify with, said Roberto Assagioli (the founder of psychosynthesis), controls us, but we gain mastery of our lives when we identify with the self.

So often the role we have played for so many years is taken away from us or no longer seems to fit. Who are we then, when the roles we have embodied for so long no longer serve us? Sometimes people feel they have lost their identity when they retire, or when illness forces them to give up their job, or even when children leave home and no longer need mothering. When Pascale died, I too had fallen into the trap of identifying with my grief and sadness: life is sad, I had thought. The challenge to bring in joy and to remind myself of what I had to be grateful for had helped me get over this. I no longer objectified my pain, colouring the whole of life with it. I honoured it when it was around, but I could also experience joy and many other wonderful feelings. It had taken Vivian's comment to make me realize this. And what I needed to remember and to work with was the knowing that I, like everyone else, am greater than my grief, greater than any role or identification I have, other than the identification with wholeness which is the self.

It was good to come to Santa Fe, this cornucopia of healing and personal growth, although I was warned from past experience not to sample too many fruits of this kind if I did not want to get serious indigestion. Although Santa Fe has become a tourist centre, it manages to keep an old-world charm, with its attractive adobe buildings, its narrow streets, its Indian market, and its boutiques surrounding and leading off the park-like plaza. Wherever one looked there were wonderful views across vast distances to majestic mountains, which the evening sun bathed in all the colours of liquid fire, gold and orange, pink and purple. For me, Santa Fe had all the advantages of city and countryside together, and was the ideal place to have a base.

Karen gave me a room, and the key of the door, to come and go as I pleased. It was a totally unexpected and wonderful gift which made all the difference to my enjoyment of the journey, making it possible for me to meet many of the people, and do several of the things that were important for me, and which would have been difficult if I were camping out or living in motels. An easy camaraderie developed between the two of us which allowed us to share our time together with a great deal of fun and laughter. If I were not out in the countryside somewhere, or visiting some pueblo or trying to track down some medicine person, I had Karen's home to myself during the day.

We would often sit together in the evening, chatting about our lives or some subject of mutual interest. Karen knew about my interest in healing, and that I had begun to explore the use of sound as a catalyst for transformation.

'Where did it all start?' she asked me.

'Well, soon after Pascale was born I got a severe case of exhaustion, and lost the use of words, and my memory. Orthodox medicine didn't offer anything helpful, so I embarked on a process of self-healing, which included meditation, and some personal growth work.'

'Surely having a baby wasn't the cause of that?' she said.

'No, of course not, but it was a contributing factor. Wally was away in the Arctic on a long expedition which he'd been planning for four years, and not long before he left I found myself pregnant. That happened to coincide with me writing a novel in the first person as a youth of eighteen. So my psyche must have felt a bit schizophrenic.

'Coupled to that, I had lots of things to do for the expedition while he was away, and of course I was looking after my elder daughter, Kari, who was seven at the time.'

'Trying to be superwoman,' said Karen.

'Precisely. I just about got the book finished when my mind decided it wanted a rest. So I couldn't think of ordinary normal words, I would forget what I was saying halfway through a sentence, and I'd very little recall when friends talked about things that we were supposed to have done together. It took me seven years to get back on form again.

'Looking back on it, I think it all really needed to happen. I've learned that we sometimes generate crises in our lives as an opportunity to grow or to awaken to our spirituality. I developed an existential crisis in the wake of my loss of words. And through the search to heal myself, my whole view of the world and the purpose for living changed.'

'For the better?'

'Yes, for the better. And, what's more, I developed a fascination with the whole process of healing and human potential, and decided to become a therapist and work with people, helping them to find their gifts and to understand and work through some of the changes that come unannounced into their lives.'

I had long wanted to visit Taos, where there are the remains of one of the finest multi-storeyed Indian pueblos. The Taos Indians have lived at or near the pueblo site for nearly 1,000 years. The drive from Santa Fe takes one through open scrub desert country for about thirty to forty miles before entering a spectacular canyon. The river which runs alongside the road in places is clear, fast, and sparkling on a sunny day, and a great place for rafting.

Beyond the canyon, the view opens up to a vast plateau terminating in distant mountains. Sagebrush grows everywhere in sight.

Modern buildings alongside adobe dwellings line the approach road for a few miles before one enters the quaintly attractive town of Taos which, like Santa Fe, is a centre for art. Narrow streets, lined with wonderful-looking shops, called to be explored but I was intent on visiting the pueblo, just a couple of miles down the road. It is hard to believe that a combination of mud mixed with sand and straw is durable enough to sustain a building of several levels, but adobe appears to be hardy enough to do this, albeit with a bit of replastering from time to time. Although some people live in the pueblo permanently, most of them live nearby and come in every day to sell their wares: jewellery, pottery, paintings and other arts and crafts.

It had been snowing for a few days and, with the following thaw, the ground was rather a quagmire when I arrived and bare of tourists, except for a handful – so I had the chance to browse and soak up the atmosphere of this ancient place. Bread ovens, covered up against the weather, squatted in front of the houses. These beehive-shaped clay ovens were a feature of all pueblos. The absence of a fire within them indicated, better than anything else, the lifelessness of the pueblo in winter. A couple of old women sat outside the ancient adobe structure, chatting in a language I could not understand. They were selling Indian fried bread, plain fare but good, the aroma of which mingled with the smell of sage from an open window. As I looked up towards the mountains that overshadowed the village, I had a brief sense of how the place must have been before ever a foreigner stood on its earth – the laughter of children running around outside, the barking and scrapping of dogs, the women baking the bread as the menfolk came in from the fields. The close-knit buildings were a symbol for the spirit of community everyone shared. Their plain walls fostered a stoic and passive resistance to forced change.

A pretty white mission church pointed into the centre of the pueblo. I was reminded how alien the invaders, and their religion, must have seemed to the Indians. From the belief in the sacredness of all life they were taught that the sacred is separate from the profane. From the belief that everyone is born whole and at one with the rest of life, they were taught that everyone is born with original sin. From a belief system that said wisdom was a stream put forth from the Great Mystery, beyond concepts, words, or form, they were taught dogma. And from a belief that one should not waste the bounty of this earth, they became witness to the despoiling of their habitat, and their great herds of buffalo made virtually extinct. I was reminded of a statement made by a young Greenlander once, talking about the effects of the missionaries: 'They took away our spirituality and gave us religion.' I wondered if this were not true also of the Native Americans.

As I looked up at the large, tiered, adobe building which used to house a whole community, I could see the straw showing through where it needed some repairs. The rooms were small, occupied as shops, where once they were family quarters. There are doors and windows now where once there were none. Risk of attack had prohibited these openings which would have been vulnerable. Entrance to the building was by means of ladders up the walls and in through hatches in the roof. It must have been exceptionally dark living inside, and claustrophobic, as there were no inside stairways to get from one floor to another. Dwarfed by the mountains behind, the pueblo was divided by a stream separating a further group of dwellings. These too were made of adobe, and housed some shops as well as people.

I wanted to take a look at Picuris pueblo on my way home and, soon out of Taos, the road began climbing steeply through wooded mountains to the hidden valley bearing its name. I knew of this place through reading a book by Beautiful Painted Arrow, also known as Joseph Rael, a very special healer, teacher, philosopher and shaman, to whom it had been home. He had written about the magic of this village, hidden among the mountains, which was alive with spirit. Picuris once housed several six-storey mud and stone dwellings, and was once one of the largest pueblos. Ancient tribes had lived in the area since as early as AD 900. Picuris played a major part in the Pueblo Revolt of 1680, and again in 1696, after being taxed to near starvation. The inhabitants abandoned the pueblo to join the Apaches in their excursions through southern Colorado, and returned in very much reduced numbers in 1706 to what is now one of the smallest pueblos.

It was sunny and warm when I drove into the village, after a wonderfully alpine drive. I had to buy a permit to walk around the village. This was a way of checking the number of visitors, and prevented too many disturbing the peace of the place. I was given a map delineating which areas were accessible and which were sacred and protected. The air was crisp and clear, which was to be expected at an altitude of 8,400 feet. All senses alert to drink in the special atmosphere, I walked around the village, up to the old ruins which had been raided frequently in its heyday by the Comanches, and up into the hills that overlooked the village. All the while, I imagined what it would have been like to have grown up in the pueblo where every rock and tree, every path and stone was invested with magic, as it had been for Joseph Rael.

In a wonderful passage in his book, *Being and Vibration*, he tells that as a child he was taught that 'we existed as pressure point activators for the sacred sites within the villages. Every twenty feet or so were consecrated points on the ground which carried special blessings.' He explains that the shrines were buried in the ground and were only visible to those with inner vision. And he claimed that as people walked through the village they activated the sacred sites with their bodies' pressure. 'The holy shrines were placed there because the vibrational essence of those holy sites would enhance the psyche of community and of each individual within the community.'

I wished I were sensitive enough to experience the energy of the land as vividly as Joseph Rael had. What I did feel in this high, hidden valley was an elixir in the air, of champagne vintage. I felt uplifted just to sit in the sunshine, on the hillside.

But, without realizing it, on my way back to the car I found myself on the roof of a kiva. This is a sacred space hollowed into the ground, reached only by ladder through an opening in the top.

There was something stirring about seeing the roof of this sacred space among people's dwellings. It underlined more than anything the spiritual nature of the people living there. As a thin cloud of smoke wafted upwards through the opened hatchway, I sent my respect with it to the Great Mystery in which we all had our being. An old gentleman stood at the door of a nearby dwelling and raised his hand in greeting. I acknowledged him silently as I passed on my way to the car, wondering at the ease with which, in special places, one need only to look to speak one's heart.

CHAPTER NINE

Standing Eagle

I WAS DELIGHTED TO FIND THAT THERE WAS TO BE A workshop in long-distance healing in Santa Fe, given by Standing Eagle, a medicine man of thirty years' experience. Described as an Apache/Ute/Yaqui healer, he had been initiated by his grandmother in northern New Mexico, and was offering initiations into healing. I was still burdened at times with grief for Pascale, and hoped that through various healing workshops and the different purification rites, I would be released of this heartache. Sometimes, seeing young girls of her age would bring floods of memories. And even though I knew better, I could not stop thinking that I would be without her forever. What would fill my days now that she no longer could? What would fill my heart? I did not talk often about these painful feelings. I preferred to include thoughts and stories about her when I was feeling happy. But, at times, I had to admit that I felt leaden. 'You must give up the notion of time,' said Karen. 'It's that which is causing you the most grief.' Maybe she was right. I should stop thinking about 'forever'.

I phoned to book a place on the workshop, which was to take place two days later, and was answered by a strong, vibrant, youthful, male voice. 'You had better come early,' Standing Eagle cautioned, 'as I'm going to have to turn lots away from the door.'

'You can't turn me away, I have come all the way from England,' I rejoined.

He chuckled at that. 'There's a form you'll need to fill in before the workshop. Where do you live?' By coincidence, Standing

Eagle was to visit somebody in the same residential park that evening. 'You can meet me in one of the other blocks in twenty minutes, if you like,' he offered.

Karen said she would come with me to show me the way. It had been snowing and the ground was icy in places. We slithered and slipped down the banks that marked the boundaries between the various blocks of condominiums, and reached the prescribed one, panting and out of breath. Standing Eagle greeted us with a serious expression, which spread to a smile after we had been chatting for some time. Loose, unbridled hair framed the long face, whose cast looked not unlike the bird whose name he had taken. His voice belied his age, which was about sixty. Lean and long-limbed, he had a gentleness to his manner which was confirmed by his soft brown eyes.

Within minutes, I felt an ease chatting to him as if we were old friends. He explained that he had been brought up in an urban area, not with a tribe, and so his training had been unorthodox. There were many things he had had to discover for himself. He had missed the support that he might have had if he had lived on the reservation, but the benefit of going it alone was the freedom it gave him to find his own truth away from any tribal pressure to conform.

'These are the things you need to bring with you to the workshop.' He proceeded to write down a list of items, such as a blanket, notebook and pen, loose warm clothing, when he suddenly burst into laughter. I looked over to see what had caused the hilarity and realized that instead of writing 'snack to eat' he had written 'snake to eat'. 'The snake is my power animal,' he explained, and I was to discover just how significant that was a couple of days later.

Standing Eagle was very welcoming to everybody when we arrived for the workshop. He asked each person, privately, what form of meditation they did, if any at all, and then explained that for today he would give a simple meditation for us all to do, which required no more than following the breath. There was no effort, no goal, just the ability to sit and do nothing. He went on to explain that in order to heal, or indeed to affect the material world, as this process would teach us, we needed to be able to harness universal energy, rather than using up our own finite physical resources. To do this, one needed to charge up the energy centres of the body, which in the Far East are known as the Chakras. He showed us a simple set of exercises, which I had learned in yoga as the Salute to the Sun, which he said was excellent for awakening these wheels of energy.

That was followed by an exercise to ground our energy. Again, it was a familiar exercise to me, but one which I needed to be reminded to do. It was evident that Standing Eagle had explored other spiritual systems than the Native American. It was good to see that he could incorporate these in his own esoteric practice. These exercises were the preliminary to being able to feel energy; not only that generated by our own body, but that of other people. And again, this was preparatory to being able to locate, and feel, the platform of energy, called the assembly point, from which one could send out healing energy, or a shield to protect someone. This was also the manner in which one could actively influence the material world in order to manifest our desires.

From friends of mine at home, I had come to realize that there was a difference between learning a technique for healing and actually being able to use it effectively. The success of the process seemed to depend on the intensity and clarity of one's intention. And this could be adversely affected by emotional and psychological hang-ups. Standing Eagle had the answer to this. First, one breathed through the mouth for as much as twenty minutes: this created balance in the body, and also acted as a purifying process. One followed this by activating the body's natural energy centres, and grounding this energy. One then meditated on the breath, creating a state of nothingness. And then one used a combination of power words to create the necessary state of mind, before one launched the intention in the prescribed manner. In doing this, one actually began a process of purging and self-healing. 'In this work you meet both the shadow and the light. This work fosters growth,' he explained. 'Expect change.' He added that there was a self-regulating safety device, an esoteric ring-pass-not, or neutralizer, in one's psyche that prevented anything from being achieved without goodwill, and that this in turn had a transforming effect on one's character.

He went on to show us how the meditative process should be followed by a hands-on-self series of exercises which would heal the body and re-balance its electro-magnetic energy. Disease occurs when there is imbalance, or blockage, of the body's energy flow and can be caused by trauma, or disharmony in the physical, emotional, mental or spiritual levels. He was a remarkably unassuming teacher and very likeable. He told us that his grandmother, although now dead, still acted as his spiritual guide. We were asked to lie down while he began an initiation in which we would call on his grandmother to assist us in finding our life's purpose. He had put on a beautifully beaded, ceremonial, buckskin shirt, which he wore with his jeans, and proceeded to drum and sing in the wonderful haunting way of his people.

We had been asked to write our spiritual name, or medicine name as it was also called, on a piece of card and place this near our head, so that he could read it aloud as he invoked the spirit of his grandmother. I had not yet been given a medicine name, but I especially liked my name to be pronounced properly, which was like the word 'marry', and wrote it so that he would say it this way. As he drummed near each of us, he spoke a message in our ear.

'Marie, may you gather completely the essence of your energy centres.'

In the break that followed the ceremony, he talked about his childhood and the fact that he had been completely open and fearless, like most children. His grandmother had taught him how to relate to nature and all her creatures without fear. He had played with rattlesnakes and never got bitten. His grandmother would keep watch and take them away after a while if there was a danger of him forgetting they were there and accidentally hurting them, when they might have struck out. He explained that wherever he went, as a youngster, he would always attract rattlesnakes. His mother, however, did not share his fascination for them and wanted to move home for that reason. Clearly, the snake was drawn to him because it was his medicine animal.

The word 'medicine' as used by the Native Americans refers to the inherent ability to promote alignment with the Great Mystery and all life. It promotes healing of body, mind and spirit. Medicine can bring personal power, protection and insight. But it is not the individual who chooses a power animal, it is the animal that makes the choice to enter into a spiritual partnership with a person. The animal may appear initially in dreams, in a vision quest, or in physical form. On occasions, a person may wish to invoke a specific animal in order to benefit from the particular lessons or energy that animal represents. Ideally, the human seeks at-one-ment with the animal so that s/he may absorb its essence, and with that, its physical and spiritual gifts. Animals, to the Native American, are as much the children of the Divine as we are, and represent spiritual principles as well as physical manifestations of the Great Mystery.

Standing Eagle said that the intent was important in healing, but that one should not be too specific in one's request. Rather, one should let spirit take care of the details. 'Spirit knows what is right,' he emphasized. By the end of the afternoon, we were all tired. It was surprising just how much energy was used in the healing process. Obviously, we were not yet practised enough to avoid using up vast amounts of our own energy in the process. This would come with time, Standing Eagle said.

'You can use this same process to influence the material world,' he explained. 'You can use it to affect the weather in your immediate locale, you can use it to bring all kinds of benefits into your life. But you have to make a practice of doing it regularly, every day, not just once in a while when you feel like it. If you practise every day, you'll find that you'll build up a great store of energy that you can use to achieve all sorts of things. It will also bring you great peace of mind.'

New habits are as difficult to continue as old habits are to stop. So I was relieved to hear that I was not the only one who had fallen by the wayside when it came to doing my daily practice. I was feeling rather guilty about this when I went to visit Standing Eagle a few days later to ask him for an interview. When I arrived, he told me that he had been writing some poetry on the computer, and asked if I would like to hear some. I said I would be delighted, and so he read some of it out to me. I was touched by the gesture, as much as by the poem, which addressed the actor within him, the player of many roles. I told him it reminded me of all the different sub-personalities that masqueraded inside our psyches. He admitted that he had worked on transforming the power and influence of some of them so that they only came on stage when invited, rather than hogging the limelight.

I noticed that there were a couple of spirit sticks lying on the table; these were used in ceremony, and I asked if he felt he was essentially Native American in his form of spirituality or if, as a result of the different spiritual disciplines he had experienced in adulthood, he felt he came from a more universal standpoint. He explained that in some ways he worked according to people's expectations.

'If by using certain paraphernalia they feel more comfortable because they're accustomed to it, I would use different sacred objects. I don't feel, however, that the latter are essential. As a medicine man, I feel I belong to more than one world. I have not been raised traditionally, and as a result I'm not so ethnocentric as I might've been. I was lucky that my parents allowed me to chose what was right for me, as I was brought up in a predominantly Catholic environment, with a Spanish mother and an Apache/Ute/Yaqui father.

'Children normally follow the mother's example. As a child, I was brought up in Colorado, and used to come to New Mexico for holidays. Coming to New Mexico was like coming home to me. This is a power centre: here everything was always enlivened for me. I never felt the same earth connection in Colorado. And so when the time came to return to Colorado after the holidays, I would get up to all sorts of tricks to try and delay us or even stop us going altogether. On one occasion I actually threw the keys of the car into the well in the garden. Then I hid in the sagebrush and told the spirits of nature to go away so that they would not be blamed for what I had done, or for making me want to stay. My parents tried to start the car without any keys. I was afraid I would have to go after all. So I went to the well, which I believed held the answer to my staying there. In fact, I fell into the well.' He tried to explain to me that it was happening in a different dimension.

'I was supported by a cushion of energy. I could feel eagle wings flapping around my head. The next moment I was on the planks of the well. How had I got up there? At the same moment, an old Indian man was seen walking down the road, quite wet, away from the well. He didn't live there, and had never been seen before or since.'

'Who was he?' I asked.

'I believe that the old man was my grandfather and that the experience happened in another dimension, even though I came out of the well quite wet.'

'Did you have other similar experiences growing up?'

'I had lots of shamanic experiences as a child. My grandmother taught me how to meditate, to sit easy, doing nothing. From this place of relaxed awareness, I floated in and out of other dimensions.'

I liked the gentle, humble energy of this unusual man. His eyes shone bright but kindly.

'Have you always been in touch with magic?' I asked him.

He answered, 'My childhood was filled with one magical moment after another. As a small child I could levitate, and I was also a worshipper of the sun. I don't know where this came from, but aged about three and a half I would get up and wait for the sun to rise. I would sit on the counter of the shop we had, waiting for the sun. I would just sit doing nothing in the meditative state my grandmother taught me. When I saw the sun I would leap into the air and remain suspended, filled with sunlight. Gradually I would drift to the floor. And I would continue doing this till I was exhausted, and then fall asleep on the floor.'

I smiled at the image. 'Did having these strange gifts make life difficult for you?'

'Well, as I was growing up, I found it hard to make sense of them, without a tribe to put them in context. Being in a tribe helps you channel these gifts in appropriate ways.'

'Do you believe, as many Native Americans do, that the origin of the Native people was from the stars?' I asked him.

'Well, you know, I've been a long time on the planet, through many lifetimes. This is my home.

'I have no desire to go to another world, or to the heaven that Christians talk about. This is where it's all happening. People journey to find God when really it is the reverse that happens. When we learn to love, and when we learn to appreciate beauty in its finest absolute godliness, then the creator comes to us. The people on this planet are beginning to become more conscious. We need to change our behaviour to the planet and not take her for granted. She's our mother. The planet's a living being.'

I listened enthralled, feeling such a sense of privilege to be talking to him. I commented that his grandmother seemed to have been a significant influence in his life.

'My grandmother,' he said with emphasis, 'planted seeds in me which sprouted when I was thirty years old. I had several ecstatic experiences then, during which I felt at one with everything, understood everything, and knew who I was. The dream state and waking state often seemed to merge. But there's a price for walking this path. It was too much for my wife to pay. I woke up one day and had to face the loss of everything material in my life.'

I made no comment as we sat in silence for a few moments. I knew that a medicine person, or healer, has often to chose between his vocation and everything else he holds dear. People who marry such gifted souls also have to make a choice, of whether to share their partners with the world or keep them to themselves.

He turned to me. 'You talk about a vision quest. Life is a vision quest. It took me a while to realize that I was meant to be doing spirit work. I hadn't followed a traditional path. There was no one to explain things to me. So I decided to go to South Dakota to do the Sun Dance with the Lakota people to get some direction in my life; to learn who I really was. Their acknowledgement of me made all the difference.' While he was with them, one day he went out into nature and asked for a sign. He had been standing on the edge of a deep ravine when he fell into an easy state of being, a state of knowing everything, a place where anything could happen.

122

'I had a strong desire to have an eagle fly overhead. And thought why not four, one from each direction? I asked for the first eagle and immediately a shadow broke the sunshine in the ravine. I felt such surprise, but I asked for another. And a second beautiful golden eagle appeared. At that moment, my ego began to intimidate me. It said I was a weakling and that I hadn't caused the birds to appear. I found myself seduced by these negative statements of my darker nature. In a state of confusion, I struggled to gain mastery over my thoughts, which were polluting my mind and preventing me from acting with the power and magic that I knew was mine. I called on the eagles again but the first two had disappeared into distant specks, and my call went in vain. It was then that I realized that I had listened to my dark side instead of trusting the power of that place of innocence.

'Remembering what my grandmother had taught me, I tuned in to the place of harmony and inner knowing and called on the eagles to return. They did, proving that I could call in four eagles, but they hadn't come in the manner I'd wanted. I was so disappointed, and returned to the Lakota camp where I was met by a medicine man and several others.

' "Do you know who you are?" the medicine man asked me.

'Dispirited, I explained that I'd called for four eagles but only two had shown up. The others laughed,and started teasing.

' "Don't you still know who you are? You're Standing Eagle," they explained. "Now you can do our ceremonies and be with us."

'Their encouragement meant a lot to me. To be accepted into an ancient lineage, which they had meant when they had given me my name, was more than I could hope for. I had people to support me and was no longer a homeless derelict. I participated in many of their ceremonies after that.'

He laughed when he described how hot the sweats were.

'People would actually get blisters from the heat. But I had an amazingly illuminating experience once. You know that before entering the lodge you are asked to say "Mitakuye Oyasin" which means "all my relations"?'

I nodded.

'That's an expression of such great wisdom, and also of a level of perception. Because, you know, I was everything at that moment of saying it: the seeds, the grass, the wind, the laughter, the water being poured into the bucket. I saw myself everywhere I looked. I was in everything. The wisdom of that perception! We see ourselves as unity with all of creation!'

I asked if he could explain what it meant to him to be a medicine man. His answer was unexpected.

'The moment I called back the eagles I had a revelation. It was a tender feeling, a realization that I was not specially skilled or trained to do what I had done. Anyone could do it. This power to influence material things is available to anyone on the planet. It's a special tool to be used for oneself and others. Long-distance healing, which you learned over the weekend, is the same principle. To have the weather be a certain way, you use the same principle.

'As a spirit man, my role is to let other people know how to do it. You don't have to be of a particular long lineage, anyone can develop the skill; but you have to practise.'

I asked Standing Eagle about the need to fast on a quest.

'Some people need to do it that way,' he explained, 'but also one should ask if a vision received through deprivation is a valid vision. I'm not into suffering. People say that you get a breakthrough out of suffering and that extreme suffering leads to ecstasy. But how long does that last? To my mind, I believe it's more efficacious and helpful to be in a state of ease of mind and body.'

It was something I had to discover for myself, but I was to find that he was not the only one who advocated a different approach to seeking visions.

CHAPTER TEN

An
Exceptional Lady

Talks With Bears phoned to say that he'd had a word with Jamie Sams and passed on a letter which I'd sent to her through him. If I was free, we could all have dinner together the following evening. He suggested a Japanese restaurant in town and invited Karen to join us. I was keen to meet this rather special lady, whose writings had inspired a deep love and respect in me for the holistic principles of the Native American philosophy and tradition. I understood that there was a great deal of diversity of practice and belief throughout the various tribes. I also appreciated that for many years Native religious ceremony had been outlawed by the US government, and that it had fallen to the medicine people and shamans to remember and protect the ancient wisdom. Already there was a revival of the tribal people's culture and spirituality, and Jamie was one of the people teaching the ancestral ways.

Maka and Talks With Bears were at the restaurant when we arrived. It had been some time since I had seen them, so there was much to talk about.

'You'll be a real born-again Indian before too long,' teased Maka when I told her all the things I had been doing.

We were joined a few minutes later by a tall, dark-haired woman of impressive stature and personality. She greeted Talks With Bears and Maka affectionately before turning a radiant smile on Karen and myself. I felt a warm tingling of the skin, and a distinct *frisson* in the air. The aura of certain healers reaches way beyond ordinary mortals and can be felt as a delicious lift to one's spirits. I found myself totally enchanted by her infectious humour and gift for telling a story.

In the course of the evening Jamie let us into the secret of a new 'divinatory' system that she had devised. She spoke about the way she had researched the symbols to be used in it, and shared much of the creative process. I knew that her new creation had not yet gone into production, and that, these days, she only did healings or readings for friends. But I had to ask her, even if she refused me, if she could possibly do a reading for me. She answered graciously, without hesitation, that she would gladly do it when she returned from a trip to New York, in about a week. I breathed a sigh of gratitude to the spirit that guided us both.

'You're doing the right thing,' said Talks With Bears after Jamie had left. 'Jamie'll set you right about your vision quest.' He could not have imagined how swift and significant would be that response.

I drove out of Santa Fe on a beautiful afternoon to visit Jamie at her home in the desert. The adobe bungalow, not unlike many of its kind in New Mexico, took one into another world beyond the front door. Cosy and comfortable, it had an abundance of unusual ornaments and sacred objects, drums, shields, rattles, fetishes, exquisite fans and crystals. I wanted to know the origin and history of everything, but managed to curb my inquisitiveness, except for a collection of totems, which Jamie explained were the dolls she had made to represent the thirteen original clan mothers – the role models for the feminine.

There was an organic energy to the dolls which were about twelve inches in height and made of bone, feathers, twigs, and other natural objects and fibres. Each had a distinctive quality, made the more compelling because they were representations, not of human beings, but rather of those archetypal and mythical figures that govern our destinies. To them we owe the intuitive, creative and receptive part of ourselves, which is common to both men and women, although, as Jamie explained, 'Women express it to a greater degree.'

While Jamie made a cup of tea, which she said was 'real tea' and brandished a packet from Fortnum & Mason to prove it, I told her of a vivid dream I had had about her the night before. The dream was the first of such potency that I could recall since I had blocked the dreaming process as a teenager. I was delighted to discover that it had some relevance to things that were happening in her life. The acknowledgement of this came as a welcome milestone on my vision quest, as it indicated that I was becoming more psychically aware.

I had brought a photo of Pascale to show Jamie, a particularly beautiful picture of her aged twelve, which totally captures her essence.

'She's beautiful,' said Jamie 'and I mean on every level. It says it all in the eyes.' She looked over at me and signalled me to sit down, indicating at the same time that she was tuning in to something. 'Pascale is a multi-dimensional being who is at this moment pursuing her soul journey in other dimensions, while overseeing your family in this cycle of growth. You know, she really didn't need to spend much time on this planet. She'd done everything she came to do.' She pondered for a while, and asked, 'Is clairaudience your strongest gift?'

'I don't know,' I answered, 'but I did hear her call me after she died.'

Jamie nodded. 'You're going to hear a lot more from her, but you need to be still, and listen.'

She went on to say with some emphasis, 'There was absolutely no pain for her, you understand? No pain.' She leaned towards me as she spoke, looking at me intently, but kindly, as if willing me to accept this.

I nodded that I believed her. The worst anguish a parent can feel is to know that a child of theirs has suffered. And it had been my immediate fear when I had first come upon Pascale after the accident.

And then Jamie said something which astounded me, but which demonstrated beyond doubt that her perception was beyond the ordinary. 'The sign of the cross you saw at her death is symbolic of the fact that she has reached Christ Consciousness.'

I sat quietly as I contemplated the significance of her statement. No one knew of the mark that had branded the angelic countenance of Pascale on her forehead. And yet here was Jamie, a virtual stranger who lived in America, not only recalling a specific detail of the most harrowing moment of my life but showing me how I could transform the painful image into one that was positive and uplifting.

She pointed out the spiritual significance of Pascale's short life and how her soul, knowing the stakes, had led her to live a life of such joy and purpose.

'You've been together many lifetimes, you know each other very well.'

The truth of her words rang like a bell in me, comforting me with its resonance. When Pascale was born, I had felt a sense of recognition, a feeling that a great love had been returned to me. As I nuzzled up to her tiny frame, I found myself saying, 'It's you. My sweet love. You're back.'

Jamie continued to focus inwardly and commented, 'You'll connect more and more with her as time goes on. She's not finished with your family. Listen for her.'

I had been told before that Pascale's influence would affect my future work, which was not yet in form. Also that she had touched many lives with her special radiance. I could accept all that Jamie had said, as it reiterated what I had been told by others. I was grateful for her confirmation of it.

She handed me a small leather pouch, tied at the neck with a drawstring, which fitted nicely into my hand. It must have weighed about 100 grams. 'Shake it well,' she said as she placed a small circular cloth on the table, 'and spread the contents on this medicine wheel.'

I held the bag reverently, feeling a pleasant excitement at the thought that I was holding a collection of symbols which could tell a story about my life and the path I was following. There were limitless possibilities to the patterns these could make on the cloth in front of me which, as the medicine wheel, represented the unity of life. And yet I could only have one throw. Somehow me, and the bag and its unseen contents, and the medicine wheel, and my fate, which would be revealed when I cast my lot, were all connected. As yet, I did not know what Jamie would say when she interpreted the lay of the symbols. But that moment and this one and the little bag I was holding in my hand were all inextricably linked.

The circle of cloth was blank, waiting for my throw. I stared at Jamie, expecting some further direction, but she laughed.

'There's no particular way to do this; just empty the contents any way you want on to the cloth.'

I caught my breath and shook the bag, scattering its load evenly around the circle. I saw, with delight, that its contents were small silver charms and miniatures of other objects made of various materials, about fifty-two in all, each of which was a different symbol. It looked like a treasure trove of beautiful little trinkets, and I gazed at them fascinated. What story would they tell of my destiny or fortune? Jamie looked them over with a practised eye and murmured to herself. I waited, my gaze flicking between her face and the spread between us. As she pointed to the different symbols Jamie explained their relevance individually, and in the context of how they had fallen. Groupings were significant, and the manner in which the symbols touched, or landed, whether face down or up.

'What's shown here,' said Jamie, 'is that there's a brand-new beginning, happening right now, which will take you beyond any of your fears or self-doubts into a state of abundance on all levels.' Her finger traced over the pattern made by the tiny silver objects on the cloth as she pointed to the symbols that spelled this out.

'You'll be taken by this particular cycle of events into a time of expansion and flowering beyond your wildest dreams. Enjoy this and be humble,' she said, looking at me directly.

I nodded, promising that I would. It all sounded wonderful but I hardly dared believe it. And yet I trusted her implicitly.

'Don't try and skip any steps on the medicine wheel,' she advised, referring to the different stages of growth on my life's journey. 'Just savour each step and it'll be delicious.'

I beamed at the prospect of my potential good fortune, but Jamie was not finished.

'Within six months you should experience a healing and realignment of your being which will bring with it a lifting of veils or masks, a removal of obstacles, and a rebirth. Don't forget to keep an atitude of gratitude and humility, so that you may see the overview of the new path that is being offered.' She went on to say that I should go at the pace at which I felt comfortable and that serenity and inner peace would follow. 'Recognize the courage you have in your heart. A new foundation is being manifested. All you have to do is reach out and take the support being offered.' She concluded with the admonition that I should not let my mind sabotage my prospects. 'Trust your personal power by going with the flow.'

I felt enormously encouraged by Jamie's words, while at the same time recognizing that scepticism or doubt could block the channels to inspiration and expression. I knew that my mind frequently held me back from the entrance to the realm of creativity and enlightenment I was seeking, and yet at times I felt so close to breakthrough. Jamie had spelled out possibilities that were accessible to me. I needed to be open to them, but I could only be open if I cleared any emotional baggage I carried with me. It was the emotional aspect of one's being that fed the constructs of the mind. I still had some clearing out to do but I felt inspired to tackle this challenge.

As I was gathering up my things to leave, I asked casually if she could suggest any foods I might take on my vision quest, explaining that I had developed a hyperthyroid condition and should not fast.

'Where are you doing your vision quest? Who's leading it?' she asked curtly.

I told her that I had hoped to do a four-day fast in California, in the desert.

She rose quickly to her feet as she gathered her breath. For a moment she seemed to be struggling to contain some emotion, but almost instantly she exploded. 'I'm sorry, Marie, but that really presses my buttons. Three women have lost their lives in this area in the last year doing vision fasts. It is totally irresponsible to expect a woman of your age, without any preparation, to be able to do it. In fact, it is criminal. You should not be doing a vision quest at all, you should be doing a healing quest.'

I gazed at her blankly.

'Why don't you do it the proper way, the women's way, and not the masculine way, which could actually do you irreparable harm?'

'I don't know how,' I protested.

Jamie sailed towards one of the other rooms. 'I am going to give you a book to read which explains it all, called *The Thirteen Original Clan Mothers*.'

'I've got it,' I exclaimed. 'That's what brought me here to see you. I want to do it the women's way. But I don't know how to go about it.'

'Right!' Jamie looked determined. 'If I set it up for you to do it here, near Santa Fe, with someone who leads women's healing quests, would you do it?'

'Of course!' I answered.

She picked up the phone and went off into another room. I felt excited and a bit nervous at the way things were happening. There was something going on which seemed beyond my control. In spite of all my worries, if I really looked at my journey, I had been led step by step to meet the right people. Did I really dare to trust it could be this easy, this synchronistic? Quests were meant to be tough and arduous, weren't they? Or were they? If I were to listen to Jamie or to Standing Eagle, it would suggest that things can happen magically, easily, without undue effort, when the timing is right.

Five minutes later Jamie came in, triumphant. 'It's done! You'll do it not too far away with someone who has trained with me. You'll sleep in a teepee on a feather mattress. It'll be a healing quest. You'll have food and water. It'll be a chance for you to nourish yourself and be nourished. That's the way you can contact your dreams. However,' she said seriously, 'you really do need some soul retrieval, you know what I mean, before you go in for your quest.'

I nodded. It was an expression which had alarmed me when I first heard it, until I read Sandra Ingerman's book about the subject in which she explained the ancient shamanic practice of healing the fragmented self. She claims that 'we all spend a tremendous amount of psychic energy looking for lost parts of ourselves. We do this unconsciously, and we do this in many different ways – generating dreams and daydreams, experimenting with numerous spiritual paths, or by creating relationships that mirror back to us our missing parts.'

Soul loss can occur as a result of trauma of any kind, accident, loss of a loved one, surgery, illness, abuse, or any sudden change in one's life situation. These, and many other traumatic events in our lives, cause a part of our essential selves to split off. The reason this happens is that by doing this we 'escape the full impact of the pain'. Soul loss can result in emotional, psychological and even physical illness. In ancient cultures, it was the task of the shaman to retrieve these parts of ourselves that had fled. Such aspects might appear as our ability to trust, our sense of joy, our ability to play, our creativity, and other vital parts of ourselves.

Jamie hinted that there were some childhood woundings to be addressed as well as the loss of Pascale. I knew she was referring to the death of an older brother when I was six; and the events surrounding my adoption at the age of four, when I had been uprooted from a family of five children in Dublin, where I was the youngest of three sisters and two brothers, and brought to a new family of six boys in Cambridge, where I was again 'the babe'.

The reasons for the disruption are not relevant to this story, although the effects of it, as Jamie implied, still needed healing. I had stored away the feelings of loss and confusion in the deepest recesses of the psyche, sensing even as a four-year-old that any sissyish feelings would be laughed at by the boys. As I grew to love my new family, there seemed no need to harp on the events that brought me to it. Only when I began my training as a therapist were the doors to the closet of repressed emotions breached, releasing some of the ghosts of the past. I understood the necessity of liberating and transforming energy tied up in grief or trauma, so that it did not seek expression in illness or neurosis, and so that one could become whole. I had dealt with painful memories as they emerged, and had felt confident that whatever remained would heal in its own time. Once in a while I would be burdened by a sense of separation, which arrived without warning but which dissipated of its own accord. Since Pascale's death, however, this had grown.

'I'll be doing a healing sweat lodge next week, which would be good for you to attend,' said Jamie. She scribbled a name and address on a piece of paper and gave it to me. 'This is the person who'll be leading your quest. She'll contact you later in the week to arrange a date for it. Meanwhile, I suggest you go to her weekly women's circle which will prepare you for it. You'll learn how to contact the clan mothers to ask them for their healing and protection.'

The thirteen original clan mothers are guardians of the thirteen lunar cycles. Their importance both to men and women is that each represents a spiritual principle, and all thirteen together represent the state of wholeness that can be accomplished when all these aspects of the Earth Mother are integrated. They were a perfect model for me to identify with on my vision quest.

'The teachings of the clan mothers are common to many tribes and were shared in women's lodges over centuries,' explained Jamie. 'Like the lodge you'll be doing your healing quest in, the medicine lodge was a place for women to retire to, where they could participate in sacred ceremony, share wisdom and teachings and be healed.'

Much of this wisdom might have been lost had not some tribespeople refused to live on reservations, where their spirituality and way of life would have been destroyed, and travelled instead to the mountains of northern Mexico for sanctuary. The history of the thirteen original clan mothers had been given to Jamie by two very special Grandmothers, Cisi Laughing Crow and Berta Broken Bow who were descended from families that made the long journey from their homeland to seek freedom. Their march was called the Trail of Tears, and took place in the late 1830s.

'They survived because they kept alive their spiritual traditions and their connection to Mother Earth,' said Jamie. The legacy which passed from these people is called the Ancient Teachings, some of which were taught to Jamie.

Jamie looked at me roguishly as I stood at the door. 'You don't need to put yourself through any more rigours. You've suffered enough losing a child. You don't need to suffer any more to get your vision.'

I nodded and murmured a sheepish, 'Thanks!'

She gave me a big hug as I left. 'We'll get you there,' she commented, adding as an afterthought, 'the safe way!'

I drove home on a cloud of joy and could not wait to speak to Standing Eagle the following day.

'It's as we both say,' he commented, 'you don't have to suffer to receive your vision. The choice is not yours as to where you do your vision quest. Spirit decides. And the guiding spirits want you to do it here.'

CHAPTER ELEVEN

Speaks
The Truth

PEAKS THE TRUTH, THE PERSON WITH WHOM JAMIE HAD arranged for me to do the healing quest, called me a few days later. She explained that her women's circle met every Thursday evening to meditate on the quality of each of the different clan mothers so that we could bring their wisdom into our lives. I would be able to attend several of these before my healing quest. She mentioned that Jamie had said I would need to do at least three days' silence before my quest to help me reach the required state of stillness. But, she explained, her group planned to go on retreat at a monastery in the desert for four days prior to my ceremony, and this would be the perfect way for me to prepare for it.

I questioned the wisdom of mixing two different kinds of spirituality on the same quest.

'Oh, but it all comes from the same source,' was her reply. ' "In my Father's house are many mansions" . . . they're all saying the same thing in essence.'

I laughed. I admired her inclusiveness. I just had not expected to be invited to prepare for a healing quest, essentially a Native American sprititual ceremony, at a Christian monastery, even if both paths shared many essential truths.

Speaks The Truth defended her decision, explaining that she chose the location not only because of its incredible beauty, but for its isolation and its purity. 'It's a power centre,' she explained, 'and was sacred to the Native Americans before it ever became a monastery. There are ancient ruins nearby that belong to the

Anasazi. It's the perfect place to prepare for a vision or healing quest and to do a winter retreat.'

Speaks The Truth's healing centre was in the hills, not far from Santa Fe. The view stretched for miles towards distant mountains beyond the city, whose lights shone jewel-like in the gathering darkness. Behind the large house, which was a sanctuary to those who wanted to reshape their lives, the land spread like a great undulating carpet to the hills behind, dotted here and there with adobe houses among the fragrant pines. I was met at the door by a smiling woman of about forty, with long fair hair and large hazel eyes, who stood about five feet two inches tall.

'Welcome, I'm Speaks The Truth.' She gave me a motherly hug before leading me through a large balconied room, hung with the colourful paraphernalia of Native American ceremony, drums, shields, rattles, masks. I wanted to stop and stare at a strikingly painted buffalo skull, but there were people to meet in the kitchen.

I was introduced to several women, of different ages, who had been coming to the sanctuary regularly for some time. There was an easy camaraderie about them, a sense that some had preoccupations beyond the present environment, an atmosphere of shared intimacies, and the challenges of change and new beginnings. After an exchange of greetings and introductions, I was offered a cup of tea and a snack before being taken to a room upstairs. We sat in a circle around a large drum which had been draped with an orange cloth. Marking the different directions were other smaller cloths: black, white, yellow, red, green, blue, to represent west, north, east, south, Mother Earth and Father Sky. A strip of orange across the lot, Speaks The Truth explained, represented the oneness of all, the unity of all. A bunch of sage grass lay on an abalone shell.

'We are working with the first original clan mother,' my host went on to explain. 'Her colour was orange, she is called Talks With Relations, and she symbolizes kinship with all life.'

I smiled to myself as I heard this. One of the intentions I had set myself on this quest was to establish a sense of kinship with the different kingdoms of nature. Once again, synchronicity seemed to be my companion. Speaks the Truth lit the bundle of sage in the abalone shell and smudged herself with the smoke, before passing it around the circle for each of us to purify ourselves in its aromatic scent.

'Smudging expands the aura by purifying it of any negative energy,' she commented.

The evening passed with us experimenting with different ways to sense the energy of another. One of these was to hold our palms a few inches away from another's to see if we could feel their vibration. I could feel people's energy sometimes as heat and other times as cold, as did some others. One or two experienced it as a tingling sensation. There was no right or wrong to this exercise. As in other areas of life, we might all experience the same situation in different ways. Following this experiment, we were invited to choose a stone from a selection our hostess had provided, and to hold it in our left hand to try and sense its energy. Everything in nature, including humans, gives off an electro-magnetic energy, which is sometimes called the aura, and some people can see this as well as sense it. I remembered Grandmother Twylah had said that one way of developing one's sensitivity was to hold a stone between two hands until one could feel a rhythm between the three. Exercises such as this helped one to develop one's psychic gifts. I had less success with this exercise and knew that I had still a long way to go in the field of sensory perception before I could attune to a stone's pulse.

After we had played this way for a while, and shared experiences and intimacies about our lives and our reasons for being there, we were led into a meditation to try and tune in to the essence of the clan mother of the first moon. Each of us had a different picture of how we experience this spirit and, on Speaks The Truth's suggestion, we drew the picture we had received, or wrote about the experience we had had in our journals. I had had an image of what seemed to be a snow maiden with a wolf for her companion. This animal, the other women suggested, could be one of my power animals or guides. Speaks The Truth said I should reflect on the qualities of the wolf, which had to do with being a pathfinder, the one who is at the forefront of new ideas, and who teaches these to people.

She went on to suggest that we meditate every day on the clan mother of the first moon and that we monitor any insights received during the week. We should make a note of any animals that might cross our paths during this time, and look out for any signs in nature that might have a message or teaching for us. I enjoyed the gentle and humorous way everyone shared their experiences and admired their courage in making some difficult changes in their lives.

'See you on Monday for the healing sweat,' some of them called as I left.

Only one thing blighted my journey in America, and that was a severe bout of insomnia which had begun several months before. Most nights I would get only three or four hours' sleep, and that after several hours' tossing and turning. The night of my meeting with the women, I fell asleep soon after two to be woken with a start at about three. As I opened my eyes I saw, clearly and distinctly, three large black cats sitting by the bed, staring at me. It was no dream. I could actually see them as clearly as I could see the furniture. There was nothing intrinsically menacing in their presence but the notion that I should be having a vision at all. This was unchartered territory for me and I was not yet ready to explore it.

Sitting up, I shouted at the apparition and waved my arms to shoo it away. The spectres fled in an instant, leaving me sitting on the bed, confused and uncomfortable. What sort of a vision quester was I, I asked myself, if I took fright at the first hint of the paranormal. In Western spirituality a distinction is made between visions that come from an astral realm, and those that come from a spiritual realm. The former are considered psychic manifestations and have a different quality to the more refined spiritual counterparts, and are prone to making mischief. This distinction was not one which bothered the Native mind, although I understood that even in these cultures, some people believed that spirits could be good or bad, well-intentioned or not. Animals were generally regarded as our teachers. But some of the visions received by well-known medicine people were fearfully powerful. I remembered Grandmother Spider telling me that on her first vision quest she'd been worried that she wouldn't get a vision, and even more worried that she would. I now knew what she meant. I also recalled how she had told me that I could protect myself from any negative energy by making a circle of stones around myself and invoking spirit, and that just to imagine doing this was enough to invoke protection.

Amazingly, I had not woken Karen. I was a bit reluctant to go back to sleep and decided to smudge the room and put a lighted candle on the shelf. I was not sure which category my apparition originated from, the psychic or the spiritual, but I strongly suspected the former, and decided I did not want it back.

The next morning I told Karen about the incident. She looked mildly alarmed. She had been looking after three black cats in a nearby flat for a few weeks, while the owner was away, and was worried that they might be disturbed by being alone so long.

'Do you think what you saw could have been the psychic counterparts of those three?' she asked.

I didn't know. I told her that the figures had looked very similar, but were considerably larger. I had wondered if there was some connection to the cats down the hall.

'We'd better do something about that room today,' she urged. 'That's not the first time something unusual has happened in there.' She went on to tell me how her own cat had been frightened out of my room, hair standing on end, some weeks previously for no apparent reason, and a friend's dog had been equally frightened. She said we should both go and get a bright new cover for the bed to brighten the room up. And she came in with the dream catcher which had been hanging over her own bed, adding conspiratorially, 'That should catch any bad spirits.' These attractive 'spider-web' objects, which were often decorated with feathers and crystals, were supposed to filter out the bad dreams and capture the good ones.

When I told Standing Eagle the next day what had happened he laughed.

'Congratulations!' he said. 'You're obviously becoming more

psychically aware. But, Marie, next time you have a vision, don't shoo it away. Ask it if it has a message for you.'

I told him I would try but that I hoped I wouldn't see anything on my healing quest that would scare the wits out of me.

He seemed very amused by my response. The visionary world had been familiar to him since he was a child. Spirits held no threat for him. Fear often generated its own images, and I wished I had his confidence and sang-froid.

'How are you, generally?' he asked, looking at me in that solemn fashion that was particularly his.

I explained that I had been suffering from insomnia for weeks on end, and asked if he had cure for it.

Once again he laughed. 'I had that for a year and a half, once. You should welcome it. It's a sign that you are learning to be in two realities at the same time, the sleeping and waking states. It's a good sign. When you've mastered it you'll feel a unity with all life, a connection. You'll not be afraid because you'll be in your power. You're learning to be in your power.'

The evening Jamie had arranged to do the doctoring lodge, as she called it, was very cold. It had snowed heavily the day previously and there was still a fair covering on the ground. As a group of us huddled around the fire, Jamie pointed out a cloud in the eastern sky which looked like a feather.

'See that cloud! That's an indication that there's an opening taking place between the dimensions right now. This is a moment when we can contact spirit more easily.' She looked anxiously towards the house where a couple of latecomers had just arrived. 'We need to go in.'

She picked up a bundle of sage and poked it in the embers of the fire.

We hopped from foot to foot in the snow in our bare feet as she smudged us, before bending low to enter the lodge. Finally Jamie crawled in, after smudging the late arrivals. There was much shuffling and laughing as we shifted first one way and then the other to try and fit everyone in. I could feel the cosiness of a body seated on either side of me, and a sense of coming together in a close bond with the other women.

Jamie sat near the entrance, the water bucket beside her as she helped steer the pitchfork carrying the hot rocks towards the fire pit. There was skill in setting them down in the right position, and it required concentration so that they did not slip off into the lap of someone sitting on the floor. I waited for the first tang of sage in the air as it sizzled on the hot rocks. And then suddenly the flap was down and we were plunged into darkness.

Jamie spoke about the intention for the ceremony. 'This purification lodge is to prepare Marie for her healing quest, and to support her in her endeavour, and it will include a healing for all of you. We'll start by going round the circle to give each of you the opportunity to introduce yourselves and say why you're here.' Jamie suggested that we use our medicine names to introduce ourselves. For those of us who did not have one, if we wanted she would request a medicine name from spirit. Some of the women had these special names, others didn't, and some even wished for a new name, believing that the lessons contained in the previous one had been completed. There was a tremendous beauty to the names received from the ancestor spirits. And even though I didn't know the other women very well, I could tell that each name was a gift in itself and symbolized some very special aspect of that person's beingness. I had no idea what my medicine name might be, and then Jamie pronounced it. 'Marie, the ancestors say that your medicine name is Sunlight Through The Trees.' I felt a burst of joy in me, and realized that the gift I held most dear to me was the joy which could transform even the gloomiest situation, just like a burst of sunlight through the trees. Remembering this name would be the most powerful way for me to connect with nature.

The rocks in the fire pit glowed red but, other than that, nothing was to be seen within the lodge. From the other side of the door flap someone spoke about her personal reason for being present, adding, 'I am Stands Tall Woman. I am here primarily to support Marie on this healing quest of hers. I ask Great Spirit that she receive the guidance and healing that she needs and that she receive her vision.' By the time it was my turn to speak, each of the women had declared that her main intention for being there

141

was to offer her encouragement and energy to me, so that my healing quest would be a success. I was deeply moved.

Jamie went on to talk more generally. 'You all know that women hold the energy for their visioning and creativity in their wombs. If any of you are unfamiliar with this concept, we'll start with some breathing exercises so that you can all learn how to energize this part of yourselves.' For the next few minutes, on Jamie's instruction, we breathed into the area of our wombs and imagined it filled with light. To mark time she played the drum, instructing us how to harness this energy by tightening the pelvic floor muscles, which would then augment the energy which we could use to create what we needed in our lives through visualization.

'It's important you try and do a monthly retreat during your menstruation,' she advised. 'That way you renew yourselves and replenish your bodies.' We sat in the warm huddle of the lodge as she spoke in the darkness to us. 'These times of retreat for women are as powerful as any vision quest, believe me. They are times to connect to the healing energy of Mother Earth . . . to sing and dance if you want to . . . to create poetry and art . . . and to give thanks and receive.' She explained that during her menses, a woman is much more psychically aware and receptive than at other times, which was why some of the tribes respected the power of women to prophecy, and that this ability to vision was used in times of trouble for the benefit of the whole tribe. She told us that the veil between the physical dimension and the spiritual one is thinned at the time of the full moon which is why this is a good time to utilize our dreams, and that if a woman were in tune with her natural cycle, she would be in tune with the cycle of the moon. She also explained that food and water were essential during this time, adding that if we ate lightly the body wouldn't try and sabotage the process.

Between each of the four rounds the flap was opened to let in air and to bring in more stones. Each new round brought a change of emphasis to the healing process. As she spoke to each person, Jamie signified things that were relevant to this particular stage of each person's journey. Each person received a gifting and a healing in line with their own unique journey and destiny.

'Marie,' Jamie began, 'you have had several Native American lives.'

I felt that much had been explained for me when she said that. It could account for the resonance I felt for the land and its Native people. I was sitting next to Jamie in the lodge when suddenly she put out her hand and touched me.

'You hold rage in your hips, Marie. It's important you clear it before your quest. I'll ask Speaks The Truth to help you with this. Today, we'll work on your heart.'

In the moments that followed, she placed one hand deftly on those areas around the heart that harbour old hurts, while the other she held over my heart area on my back. Gently, but with firm pressure, she loosened the knots that stored emotion as she kneaded them with her hand. As she homed in on those places to which memories had been relegated out of everyday consciousness, and to which the body had become host, a wave of neglected childhood feelings burst over me. The sobs of a child blurted from somewhere deep within me, utterly distraught. Jamie urged me on to release the emotions that the inner child had been unable to express at the time of its dislocation and grief.

Purging damaged emotions is never an easy task. Part of oneself baulks at the discomfort and embarrassment of it. It takes an act of will to expose oneself so nakedly. A strong part of me urged escape from such defencelessness, but an even stronger, wiser part coaxed me to stay and be shriven.

'We all have a wounded child inside us,' said Jamie. 'It takes courage to deal with such powerful feelings.'

As I had begun to voice my own from the depths within me, Jamie had urged the other women to use the opportunity to purge themselves of the dark feelings that they clung to. This way too they could support my process. Encouraged by her, the women voiced their feelings alongside my own. Their voices were muted as they began to sound into the cushions they had brought in with them. Harsh and ugly at first, the clamour of disowned feelings bound us together in a fierce embrace, until, quite suddenly, emotion spent, it stopped.

'How do you feel, girls?' asked Jamie as she released me from her embrace.

'Wonderful! Energized! Good! Warm!' came the replies.

Jamie laughed.

I knew myself that nothing clears unwanted energy better than a good howl.

Purification rites, by their very nature, bring one's personal drama to the surface. As each of us around the circle spoke about what was most present for us, Jamie showered us with a scoop of cold water. We gasped, shocked out of old mindsets and responses by the suddenness and unexpectedness of the cold shower. Then came laughter as the dousing acted as a booster rocket to our senses and emotions, catapulting us into a deliciously vibrant and joyful state of mind.

By the fourth round, when Jamie led us in some sacred chants, a healing had worked its magic on all of us, leaving us calm and purged, and immensely grateful. Jamie told us to look towards the roof of the lodge to see the tiny specks of light that were the the spirits' way of showing themselves. I could barely distinguish these, but as we stepped outside on to the frosted earth, the velvet night sky seemed crusted with diamonds.

CHAPTER TWELVE

Desert
Sanctuary

A CALL AT FIVE IN THE MORNING WOKE THE EIGHT OF US who were to go on retreat. Speaks The Truth had invited me to stay at the house the night before. I felt at ease there and had become very fond of the women in the healing circle. An unusual rapport had developed, in spite of the relatively brief time we had spent together. There was a sense of kinship, and an excitement had built up around the idea of going off into the wilderness, in company with each other, to find ourselves. Not all the residents would be coming on retreat, but everyone joined us in the living room to show their support.

Speaks The Truth told us that this was a North Direction Retreat, which meant that we would be focusing on the qualities inherent in this place on the medicine wheel. 'In Native American mythology,' she explained, 'the north's the place of wisdom and gratitude. It's represented by the buffalo, the "holder of abundance". We'll invoke the qualities of this archetypal principle, but we'll also look to the personal themes that colour everyone's individual quest.'

She placed the Sacred Path Cards, the Medicine Cards, and the Lakota Sweat Lodge Cards on the table. We were to draw five cards from these combined decks to put us in touch with the concepts we were to bring to our awareness during our retreat. Each card represented a spiritual principle or learning. Their message was extraordinarily apposite to everyone's journey.

As each person selected a card, and read their message, there was a deep sense of wonder and appreciation. The cards had an uncanny way of highlighting important truths for each person. As we drew each card we placed it in one or other of the different directions on the medicine wheel. Each of these cardinal points added a further dimension of meaning to the card's teaching. I pulled the beautiful Mother Earth card which I put in the north, the place of wisdom and renewal. 'In the near future you will find yourself giving birth to a new idea, beginning a new enterprise, or starting life anew in some way.' Wasn't that what Jamie had said?

The card for the west, which is the place of inner knowing, was Moonlodge, where one went to meditate or do a retreat. And wasn't that exactly what I intended? In the east, the place of enlightenment, I pulled the card for Power Place, which suggested I should find a place of power, a place that charged me with its energy, in order to empower myself. And was I not going to such a place in the desert? In the south, the place of the child, the place of trust and innocence, I pulled the Bison Nation Man which signifies attainment of one's highest goals. The card's message said that my past actions and faith had led me to the place of attainment. And that I would experience this achievement on both the physical and spiritual levels. Could I dare to believe that I was soon to 'arrive' at that place of fulfilment?

Finally, in the centre, connecting it all, I pulled the Crow card, which signifies sacred law, the ability to know the unknowable mysteries of creation. The message said, 'Crow is the shape-shifter. Crow can bend the laws of the physical universe.' I believed in magic, but I could not yet see myself as a magician. There was, however, a magic in life. And this I determined to seek continually.

What these cards illustrated was the importance of looking for one's wisdom and gifts, one's sense of self, and one's power through the feminine, through the moonlodge or the place of retreat, and through one's connection with the earth. They asked that I trust in the reward for endeavour, and that I be aware that there was more to life than is first apparent. They pointed to a level of consciousness which, when achieved, equips one to do things that on an ordinary level look like magic. The cards invited each of us to enter deeper into the mystery.

It was an excited but sleepy group of travellers who took to the van and Jeep. Five of us piled into the latter, driven by Speaks The Truth, while a spirited, big-hearted woman called Susan drove the pick-up. The early sun bathed the desert landscape in a soft pink as we drove out of Santa Fe. After a couple of hours' drive we turned off the road on to a dirt track. Sagebrush covered the red desert wilderness. The flatness of the immediate terrain was dominated by wondrous vermilion rock formation in the middle and far distance. We had to drive thirteen miles to reach our destination in the isolated canyon. Deep ruts scoured the track. We had been warned that entrance or exit to the canyon was only possible early morning or late evening after rain or snow, for, during the day, the sun's heat turned it into a quagmire.

The going was tough for the Jeep but even worse for the truck. We lurched and juddered over the ruts at a snail's pace for several miles, before eventually rounding a bend to see ahead of us the beautiful chapel of the monastery at the foot of spectacular cliffs. The adobe colours of the buildings reflected the red of the earth and the rocks. The church's lofty beauty harmonized with nature's scale and form. We were to discover that its tall windows focused the gaze towards the rocks' magnificence, creating a resonance between the inner temple of the church and nature's outer sanctuary. There was a natural grandeur to the canyon, coupled with a profound silence, with made one hold one's breath. This was indeed a power place. To stand anywhere in the canyon was to be in thrall to a pantheon of spirit faces that peered down at one from every level and aspect of the rocks.

'The rock people talk,' one of the monks was to confide in us. So even they succumbed to nature's charm. It felt good to know that they too could commune with the nature spirits.

The guest house was separate from the monks' area and was the first building we reached. We had been asked to wait in the common room. The rectangular room had a fireplace at one end, faced by a sofa and coffee table, a larger dining table and chairs further down, and a kitchenette at the far end. Flowers graced both tables. While we were waiting, Julie explained how we would spend the next four days.

'Meals will be shared in the monks' dining room, where we will eat in silence. Part of the day you'll be on your own and free to roam wherever you want. You need to be aware of the nature of the terrain, and realize that there's always the possibility of seeing snakes or wild animals.' The mud made walking difficult and the monks had advised against climbing the cliffs, as the surface was slippery at this time of the year.

I could not help thinking how different this high desert was from its lowland counterparts. At 6,000 feet, a hardy scrub grass, sagebrush, and pinyons flourished. I had expected sand instead of the red earth, and had not expected its surface to be so soft. Even walking from the guest house to the car park was enough to cover one's boots in a thick layer of red clay.

After a little while a smiling Vietnamese monk appeared and introduced himself as the janitor. 'The bedrooms are all along there, with two up on the next level. You're now free to occupy them.'

We trooped past the small cells that surrounded two sides of a courtyard, and drew lots for each room. There was very little difference between them. Each had one or two beds, a small table and chair, and a wardrobe and wood stove.

We were very grateful to the monks for sharing this special place with us, and for allowing us to honour the ancient wisdom in our own way, which was different to theirs. As Speaks The Truth said, we needed to see the value in all paths, and not judge others for believing differently from ourselves.

'It's not the outward form that's most important, but the deep connection one has to Great Spirit,' she said. 'We all need to balance the male and female principles within ourselves.' She advised us to leave behind symbolically anything we did not need any more. This was a chance to let go of unworkable habits and attitudes. 'Let go of your expectations,' she urged. 'They're so small compared with what spirit can give us if we open up. This is a time to get closer to our essential selves. When you go out into the countryside on your own, think of the walks as medicine walks. Allow the world of nature to be your teacher, and you might find that it takes you closer to your true identity.

'The medicine people believe that all wisdom is camouflaged, unless one believes in an invisible world. And this other world only becomes visible when we've learned to function with an open heart. Remember, the place of the north is a place of healing and gratitude. That healing comes to those who don't blame life's experiences but who give thanks for their teachings. Native American wisdom encourages people to accept all of life's experience as opportunites for growth.'

I liked her relaxed approach to things, and felt sure that this retreat would be a valuable preparation for my healing quest.

That evening, as we climbed the stairs to the balcony outside Speaks The Truth's room, we saw, silhouetted against the moonlit sky, the face of a beautiful maiden. The rounded forehead, the chiselled nose, and the delicately shaped lips above a neat chin, expressed a quality of perfection intrinsically feminine, brought into relief by the light of the moon. This was not a statue or anything that had been chiselled by hand, but simply the natural contours of the cliffs which formed the image. The scene reflected the symbolism of our inner quest: the feminine, moontime, and retreat. A feeling of harmony settled on us as we looked outwardly at an image which expressed the essence of what we held inside.

It was already February and the second moon cycle which represented the clan mother known as Wisdom Keeper, whose teaching was to honour the truth.

'She's the protectress of sacred traditions, keeper of the stone library, and the earth history,' said our guide.

Once again, synchronicity played its part in the choice of places for retreat. The full moon predisposed us to attuning to greater levels of awareness, and the predominance of rock opened up the wisdom of the 'rock people' to us – the keepers of ancestral knowledge. The first because it expanded one's psychic sense, and the second because, as Jamie Sams had often explained, stones record events that happen in their vicinity.

Speaks the Truth suggested that we each find a flat stone which we could hold over our stomach to help us attune to earth energy. Each day we were asked to look at the gift of wisdom through a

149

different aspect of our personality, suggested by one or other of the positions on the medicine wheel. The first day we looked at things from the position of the east, the place of enlightenment and clarity. Illumination, it was suggested, was found through honouring each person's right to have their own personal truth. The voice of truth, it was pointed out, was not found by following others, but could be found within one's own spiritual essence.

The second day, being the place of the south, the place of the child, trust, and innocence, I decided to use my childlike curiosity to explore our surroundings. Strangely enough, I felt very vulnerable and nervous as I set out. We had been told by one of the monks that bears rarely came to this part of the canyon, but I could not rid myself of the fear of coming face to face with one, as had happened to one of the group on a previous vision quest. I scanned the ground for snakes as I prodded around for a good stone on one of the rock tips. And I felt uncomfortably threatened all the time I was away.

That evening, Speaks The Truth gathered us together to talk about aspects of our childhood. This brought up some emotional memories, and she remarked, 'Most people have areas of their lives that they would prefer to forget, but which often scarred or wounded them in some way,' and she suggested we work on clearing some of this material out of our systems. She had been instructed by Jamie to focus on me to extend the healing she had begun in the sweat lodge, as she felt I still had a significant package of grief from childhood, as well as my more recent loss, that needed to be moved on before my quest.

We began with some exercises for women to loosen the hips, rolling them in a figure of eight first one way then the other. One of the women who did body work showed us some pressure points around the hip area to release tension that could build up over years. Speaks The Truth said she wanted to guide us into a process to cleanse ourselves of any negative energy buried in the body's tissue, when all of a sudden she seemed to be right next to me. We had done a couple of stretching exercises on the floor when she told me to lie on my back, with my knees bent and my feet on the ground. Holding my knees she swung them in circular motion first one way then the other. I felt a hypnotic rhythm develop, followed by a rising tide of emotion. I heard her call to the other, 'Gather round, girls.'

She kept the circular motion of my lower limbs, and said, 'Marie, the time has come for you to deal with what remains of your childhood grief. It does you no good to hold on to it. It actually inhibits your growth. What I want you to do is to gather all the grief from childhood into your womb, and then I'll ask you to release it.'

The pace of her manipulation quickened. I felt myself rocked like cork on a sea of emotions. As memories flooded into consciousness, her ministering became more urgent.

'Draw them into your womb.'

A tide of memories ripped through me of separation and loss.

'Draw them into the womb,' she urged again.

I could feel the women gather round me, holding me, stroking me. Someone cradling my head, others holding my hands, soothing and caressing me, their love pouring into me. I focused my intent on what she had asked of me, as my body heaved with the waves of childlike emotion that I tried to contain. Sounds of a baby blurted out of me from a time long past. As I gathered its energy into the womb, my body rocked again, this time with a different motion.

'Let it go, Marie. Let it go.'

I could feel the concentration of all the feelings in my womb, and then it began to move downwards, like a child about to be born. A heave, and the energy was dissipated.

'That's it, you've done it, Marie. Well done.'

I lay for a few moments with energy spent. Speaks The Truth put her hands on my heart, and massaged it in soft round strokes.

'Now, Marie. It's time for you to let go of the even bigger hurt. Its time for you to release Pascale. Let her go. Your grief holds her back.'

Her words cut me to the quick. I would never hold Pascale back. I would never do anything to hurt her. How often had I tried to release her? How many times did I have to do it? Anger and grief racked me as once again Speaks The Truth urged me to concentrate the feelings into the womb. I thought back to the magic of her birth, the recognition of such a great love returned to me; her second birthday in Greenland with the Inuit; her joy, her fun, her bubbling laughter; riding her bike and the poem she wrote about it; her love of dolphins; her fifteenth birthday and the promise of more to come; singing her first solo – and what a voice, how she'd surprised us all with its power and richness. The fifth form and studying for exams; campaigning for animal rights; and that course work she lost on the computer, the tears, the anguish, the starting all over again, another 13,000 words to be rewritten the same day she died. The excitement on her face as we talked about the sixth form college we hoped she'd go to, waving to her at the door as we went for a walk . . . Returning an hour later to find her dead. Never to have another hug. Never to share another tender moment. A wail escaped me. Sobs answered from either side of me. Someone caressed my face, others my arms and legs. I could feel the love of the women around me, willing me to do whatever was needed to be healed.

'Bring it into the womb.'

My body racked again as I strove to release every shred of attachment. The cord that had bound us together seemed connected to each and every cell in me. Painstakingly I released these, sometimes separately, sometimes in clusters. As I pulled them away, I felt as if they tore part of my flesh away with them. Speaks The Truth coaxed and comforted, begging me to focus it all in the womb. As I did this there was a burst of pure visceral energy.

'That's it. Let it go, Marie. Breathe! Imagine it's a baby you're releasing to the light.'

I breathed as if I were in labour, pressing down to release the pain, visualizing it as a child being born. Transmuting the anger, grief and loss into a symbol of joy. The body responded to a rhythm of its own. Symbolically, Debbie held out her hands to receive the 'child' of my effort. I was asked to hold it to my chest, and release it, when I felt ready, to the light. I lifted my hands heavenwards to demonstrate my intent. The healing I had waited for had happened. Inside, I had ached for a company of women to surround me with their understanding and their love, to create a ceremony that would integrate my scattered psyche and heal my body. I had had to come to New Mexico to find these women. As I looked up at their smiling but tear-stained faces, I felt the deepest gratitude and affection.

For an hour or so afterwards, we sat around in a cosy snug. We were all exhausted and slightly overwhelmed by what had happened. I knew a profound healing had taken place. I also knew that it had been specially hard for one or two to witness. In any group, one person can channel the emotions of the others. Although I had been dealing with my own grief, I had released the unexpressed hurts of others. I thanked Speaks The Truth, and was surprised when in return she thanked me.

'You've done something for all of us,' she remarked. 'You carried the energy for the whole group. To a certain extent, we've all been healed.'

The following day we agreed to spend in silence. I felt relaxed and calm. The focus for the day was the west, the place of inner knowing. People disappeared in different directions throughout the day. This time when I went out walking I felt at ease, and without any fear. I followed a stream, revelling in the natural beauty of the scenery. I made my way beneath the cliffs. Here and there, the red earth was splashed with a wonderful greeny turquoise from copper. Desiccated trees lay in spectacular, twisted formulations in the ravines. I found myself a perch on one of the rocks and sat and absorbed the tranquillity.

That evening we discussed the events of the previous night. The sense of intimacy had deepened in the group. We shared our feelings about our relationships with our parents, and what it meant to be a parent ourselves. A tenderness had developed between us all, a trust, and a sense of special kinship. Someone dreamed that we had known each other in a previous lifetime when we had all been monks!

On the fourth day we focused completely on the north as a place of renewal, a place of quiet, where we could find answers to vexing questions, and where we could resolve issues in our lives. There was a sense in the group that people were only just beginning to explore their inner space and that they needed more time. The beauty of the place had worked its magic on them, however. I noticed that everyone's features had softened, they were more at ease and had lost any tension they had brought with them.

Thursday was our last day, and we decided we would go for a group outing. We asked one of the monks if he would guide us, and he agreed to take us to a side canyon.

The journey to the hidden canyon was an assault course in places, as we braced ourselves against rocks, inching our way across deep pools, up over steep banks, along narrow water-courses, under overhanging rocks. We travelled most of the way in silence, drinking in the beauty of the canyon walls, and the stillness. We had travelled a good hour before we were blocked by water which we could not get across. We returned at a slightly higher level than we had approached, and arrived home tired, muddy and very hungry but with a feeling of deep thankfulness in our hearts: ready for the return journey to Santa Fe and the bustle and tension of normal life, but changed utterly.

CHAPTER THIRTEEN

Beautiful
Painted Arrow

THE TOWN OF BERNALILLO IS ABOUT AN HOUR'S SCENIC
drive through mountain and mesa from Santa Fe, and is
situated in a broad valley on the east bank of the Rio
Grande. A farming and trading Anglo and Hispanic community
shares space with the Native American population which
inhabits the modest dwellings in the section of the town known
as the Reservation.

I had decided to look for Joseph Rael, also known as Beautiful
Painted Arrow, a Ute/Pueblo Indian, master storyteller and
powerful shaman, best known for the use of sound as a tool for
healing personal and planetary disharmony, as well as for the
development of insight and spiritual awareness. Schooled in the
arcane wisdom of the Tiwa tongue, an ancient language of
unknown origin which saw everything as metaphor and which
had multiple meanings to each word, he learned as a child that
'life is the visionary unfolding of the Great Mystery' and sought to
relate everything to this concept and to teach this to others when
he became a man. It was said of him that he had the soul of a
mystic, 'one who had merged with the heart of God', and that
being in his presence could exalt one to a higher level of
awareness.

From his writings I learned that he was able to travel between
the seen and unseen realms with ease, and often found himself in
alternate realities when he least expected it. As a child he had
psychic abilities and could see beyond ordinary reality. And he
sang to the tracks of the animals he sought in the mountains, and

when he came upon them they would stop to look at him with curiosity, neither having any trace of fear.

To the Tiwa, Joseph's people on his father's side, everything was sound, everything was vibration. This was a teaching of the Far Eastern masters too, and a sentiment equally expressed in the statement, 'In the beginning was the Word'. Tiwa also states that, 'everything is made up of principal ideas, and for each idea there is also a sound.' This too echoed an ancient Eastern philosophy and was nowhere more evident than in the healing of the body with sound. I had learned that every part of the body has its own harmonic. When this harmonic is disrupted disease occurs. And one way of restoring balance and health is to sound the correct harmonic vibrations into or near the body. I revelled in the universality of what I was learning. And it was because Joseph demonstrated a universal wisdom in his teachings that I was anxious to meet and learn from him.

I searched in all the likely locations for notices about his teaching programme in Albuquerque, Santa Fe, and Bernalillo to no avail, and then I considered the pros and cons of making a visit to his home. I had a rough idea of his whereabouts, namely that he lived in the Reservation, but I would have to comb its streets for his trademark: the oval sound chamber he had reportedly built in his garden. This was one of twenty-five such edifices he had constructed around the world in which people could chant for peace, but would I recognize it or even see it from the road? Landing on him unannounced was not my favoured ploy, but I was on a quest far from home and I felt the intrusion might be excused in the circumstances.

I drove slowly through the Reservation, past trailers and small prefabricated dwellings. I was disappointed when I finally stopped in a quiet road to have noticed nothing that resembled my idea of a sound chamber. I glanced idly out of the window. The entrance of the bungalow opposite seemed a bit fancier than the others. And then I saw what I was searching for: a large wooden sign hung over the gateway which read 'Beautiful Painted Arrow'. There behind it was the curved wall of what must be a sound chamber. I was thrilled. It did not matter that no one was in the first time I called. I knew where Joseph lived, and I could come again another day.

My first glimpse of Joseph was several days later in the reflected glow of the ceremonial fire in a corner of his garden. I had arrived early in the evening, having been told by his partner the day before, when I had visited, that he would be holding a sweat lodge ceremony every week for a while, and that I was welcome to attend. While standing around the fire with several others I overheard someone talking about an initiation that Joseph would doing in a couple of weeks' time. My ears pricked up when I heard it was an initiation into the feminine. The feminine is the wellspring of our gifts and talents; it corresponds to the right side of the brain, which is the intuitive, creative, and spiritual aspect of our natures. It is the part that sees things holistically; the inclusive, nurturing and visionary part of ourselves. To know the feminine was to know one's gifts and purpose.

I watched Joseph as he spoke to other people; a man of slight build and medium stature nearing sixty. What was it about the medicine people that so demanded attention? Was it the vitality in the eyes, the stature they exhibited whatever their height, or the gentle but powerful presence that gave one a feeling of awe? Maybe it was the combination of wisdom, humour, and attentiveness that was so engaging, or maybe the magnetism that came from their obvious familiarity with other realms. Whatever it was that charmed us, like a touch of magic it held us in thrall.

'Are you coming to the initiation weekend?' a young woman asked me.

'I hope so,' I answered.

Somewhere deep inside me I knew that it was important for me to do this initiation. For among those things already mentioned, the feminine is the place where we can find and heal the lost parts of ourselves.

It was another beautiful day with blue skies and barely a cloud when I started out for Bernalillo from Santa Fe for the initiation ceremony with Joseph.

'Come inside,' Joseph called from the oval-shaped adobe building in the garden as I arrived. It took a while for my eyes to adjust to the dimness of the room. A wooden seat circled the wall on which were four masks that each mouthed a silent 'o' at the four directions. In the centre of the floor was a fire pit which had been partially covered with a wooden lid to allow a space in the middle for a person to stand, as we would do later.

I felt a sense of great privilege to be in this sacred space. Joseph described the sound chamber as a caretaker that could help us to gain access to wisdom from an ancient source. Acting as a mouthpiece of the higher mind it amplified the resonances that we need to live a balanced and harmonious life. In building sound chambers round the world his intention was to create a circle of continuous resonance which was fed by the chant of willing volunteers. I cast a quick glance around the room.

On the floor to one side was the paraphernalia of a ceremonial chamber: smudge sticks, cedar, tobacco, a drum and rattle. On this occasion there was an unusual addition: two tins filled with what looked like red and white paint.

'Tell me a bit about yourself,' Joseph invited as he gestured me to sit.

I explained my reasons for being in the States, the need for a rite of passage as well as the desire for a vision or healing quest.

He began to talk about Pascale and the child that she had been as if he had known her well. 'You must look at her life as if it were a metaphor,' he said. 'She had so totally learned what she had come to learn.' He shook his head as if in disbelief as he focused on his inner vision. 'She hadn't needed to incarnate,' he explained, 'but she came to sow seeds which are now ripe. She is responsible for your being here. You'll see her again.'

I felt a keen gratitude. I had not expected him to comment on Pascale.

'About this initiation,' he continued. 'What I'll be doing is awakening latent gifts held in the gene pool, and connecting you with energy of parallel realities. The timing is right for you. With these gifts comes enormous protection from spirit. You'll be able to appear and disappear. If an accident happens, you'll be able to move your beingness out of the way.'

I raised my eyebrows and he acknowledged my scepticism.

'Let me explain. This is not the best example but it'll do. If you were in New York and a building fell on top of you you'd be able to relocate yourself 500 yards down the road.' I must have still looked unsure for he continued, 'Believe me, this is not something I have read about in books and practised a few times, this is my actual experience. You may feel doubtful, but trust me.'

I thought back to Joseph's grandfather whom I'd heard had walked through walls. I was sure it was possible. I mean I did believe that some people could bend the laws of the physical universe. But they were special. It couldn't happen to me.

Joseph said, 'By June, in four months' time, you'll have a sense of what has happened here.' People started to arrive outside but Joseph kept talking. 'The ceremony requires that you paint your hands, face and feet with one or other of the coloured paints. You'll then go into the sweat lodge which'll be very hot, after which you'll come out into the cold and shower. This way you'll experience the polarities of heat and cold which are necessary. You don't have to understand it for it to be effective. It's all related to metaphor.'

There were twelve aspirants. They were mainly women and had come mostly from other states in the US. I sensed that many of them worked in the caring professions. A few minutes were given over to introductions when we each explained why we'd come. Everyone appeared to be in some transition phase of their lives.

'One reason we're all here,' explained Joseph, 'is that we all agreed before incarnating to meet here as a family to learn about higher consciousness and share this initiatory experience. In order for you to understand some of what we are doing you need to know that everything is metaphor. There's more to the body than the body is, just as a tree is more than a tree, and a cloud is more than a cloud. Each is a metaphor for a spiritual principle or idea, and it's important to know that metaphor has multiple meanings.'

He went on to talk about sound, the sacredness of the Tiwa language, which was his father's tongue, and which was steeped in magic and metaphor.

'All the gifts of God are in language,' he said. 'The five vowels are themselves the entry or connection to spiritual principles. When we sound them we call in or invoke those principles.' He stopped for a moment and pointed to a flip chart on which was drawn a circle with a line intersecting it diagonally. The date 20 March abutted the point at the top of the circle where the line joined it. At the lower intersection was marked the date 20 September. Between March and September the half-circle was marked 'summer people', the other half 'winter people'.

'Look to where your birthday falls,' said Joseph, 'and you'll know whether you're a summer or winter person. When you've changed your clothes, winter people should paint their hands, face, and feet with white paint; summer people with red paint.'

When we were ready, we stood around the fire pit in a circle, winter people to one side, summer people to the other. Joseph beckoned the winter people, in turn, to paint up, before inviting each one to step into the earthen fire pit which was filled with water. As each person stood in the centre, the others chanted a long 'o' sound.

Joseph had explained that the 'o' was to do with innocence, with the direction of the north on the medicine wheel, which represented wisdom, and it also had to do with the spiritual body. Chanting, according to Joseph, 'implants in the psyche the basis for the new, and fine-tunes the physical body for both spiritual and mental growth'. I could not understand exactly what was happening except that some alchemy was in process that would work its magic beyond the level of my mind to grasp it. I felt a curious satisfaction as I painted myself with the red paint. There was something primal about the ritual which spoke to a deep place in myself. As I did it, it seemed to break the bonds that tied me to any conventional mindset. When it was my turn to stand in the muddy well, I closed my eyes to feel the impact of the resonant chant. For a moment it seemed as if I was the sound itself. A tap on the shoulder marked the end of my time and I hurried across the chill space between the peace chamber and the sweat lodge.

The person tending the fire made me walk anticlockwise

around the domed tent before entering. The stones had already been placed in the centre pit and I felt the clay paint caking on my face in the heat. People sat silently, their attention inward. I sensed the response to the occasion was one of reverence and humility. Deeper than this was a gratitude for a gifting one could not truly comprehend but which one could nevertheless feel. As simple as the procedure had been, and as unusual the metaphor, I felt I had experienced something profoundly significant. I felt a wholesomeness spread outwards from within me and a conviction that, on some very essential level, I had come home.

The ceremony in the sweat lodge was brief and simple and different from normal purification rites. Joseph prayed out loud and poured water on the stones, sending a hot steam around us. Then one by one we were directed to leave the lodge and wash off the paint in the nearby shower. When we had changed clothes, Joseph offered us two ceremonial foods which he said would anchor the new consciousness that had been awakened within us. We ate this offering in silence, from the palm of our hands, savouring their taste and significance, before adjourning for the meal we had all contributed to.

That afternoon, Joseph spoke of the importance of names and the gifts inherent in them. Names, he said, were God-given, for within them were contained the purposes for our incarnation. With uncanny accuracy he reeled off the attributes of each person in the group. Those talents we recognized in ourselves we acknowledged as he listed them. Others that we had not yet realized we owned we let sink in to our consciousness. 'There is no one-upmanship here,' said Joseph. 'You're all equally gifted, though your talents and purposes may be quite different'.

There was time to ask questions before we retired for the evening and so I asked what metaphor insomnia represented, a condition which I was still suffering from.

'Insomnia is about becoming more aware of oneself,' he explained, 'but would you like it to end?'

'Yes, please!' I answered, to the laughter of the group.

'Well, as a matter of fact, the process here today should have resolved the problem, if you could call it that. You have actually been healed of it already, though you didn't know it. This process often has useful side effects.' He laughed. His prediction was to become true by the end of the week.

The following morning we met again. This time there was no ceremony; instead Joseph talked about the amazing properties of sound. He explained that the Native Americans were the keepers of an ancient wisdom which it was now their duty to share. Within each tribe there were clans which were in reality esoteric schools. His own Tiwa tradition excelled in the use of sound, whereas another tribe might be gifted in prophecy. He emphasized the power of thought, the fact that it was energy and that what we thought became our reality. 'On this plane of existence which is called perceptual reality, what we see is what we believe and what we believe is what we are. And what we have been learning about this weekend, and experiencing, is a resonance, an esoteric knowledge which cannot be known by the five senses.'

He told us some wonderful stories about his childhood and the influence of his grandfather on his life. My favourite story is the one he recounted of the time he saw his grandfather walk through the wall of the adobe dwelling and walk back again. Joseph, having been taught much about magic and mystery, assumed that he should copy his grandfather.

'Shall I do that now?' he asked.

'Find something different to do. I've already done that,' replied the old man.

Joseph explained the lesson here in this way. 'Remember everyone is an aspect of ourselves, everyone's achievement is our own. What my grandfather was suggesting was that when one human being makes a breakthrough in consciousness, as he had done by walking through walls, there is no need for anyone to repeat his action. Once one human being can do something on the planet, the potential is there for everyone to do it.'

I had a sense he was exhorting us to enjoy our gifting and find new ways of putting this into practice, in the service of others. And I wondered how the talent of seeing with X-ray eyes, appearing and disappearing, and eating light in place of food, which were all part of the gifts he said would be awakened in us, would be put to use in the future.

I drove home immensely contented. The qualities that had been awakened in me were hard to relate to. What was important was that I felt something meaningful had shifted within my psyche. I had become aware through Joseph of the mystery and miracles we had still to discover. Metaphor, which he called 'a resonating energy of the Great Spirit', was the key to seeing meaning and magic where there appeared to be none. I also knew that I did not need to look outside myself now for guidance or inspiration. Everything was contained within. I had already been taught how to tap this, I just needed to practise. My healing quest was to start this evening, and I was ready for it.

Healing Quest

WINTER VISION QUESTS ARE A RARITY. THE challenge of isolation, fasting, and inner journeying is tough enough without the potential dangers of sub-zero weather. Healing quests, equally, avoid this time of year so as not to put an added burden on the seeker. The only reason Speaks The Truth had set up a healing quest for me now was because I had limited time in which to do it. But as she and several other medicine people had emphasized to me, the quest was not primarily about deprivation, but about seeking insight for oneself and others. Gifts were never sought only for oneself in the Native American tradition, but so that everyone might benefit. Losing a child had been deprivation enough for me, I did not need to suffer any more, they insisted. What I did need, however, was a nurturing, healing quest which would symbolically release the past and bring its own insights.

The gods smiled on me from the bluest of skies as I set out early in the morning for my quest. As Jamie Sams had emphasized to me, no one should go on a vision quest without the supervision of a responsible, trained person. On women's quests, the medicine man or woman would visit the aspirant at least once a day to make sure everything was all right. I felt my heart leap with a strange joy when I caught sight of the teepee Speaks The Truth had set up for me, on a slight rise, among the cactus- and pinyon-covered hills near her home, that were so much a feature of this high desert landscape.

I do not know what it is about the teepee that so touches my heart, but every time I see one, I feel a sense of wonder and wellbeing and security. Its tall poles were festooned with red and black ribbons that fluttered out over the white cone-shaped tent. The red symbolized the south, the place of the child, the innocence and openness with which the seeker should go into the dark, the cave of the unknown, the place of the west to discover the true self. The white of the covering was the colour of the north, the place of wisdom and gratitude, and the opening faced the east, the place of illumination. Each direction was represented by an animal: in this tradition, the coyote in the south, the bear in the west, the buffalo in the north, and the eagle in the east. As I approached, I saw that there were three women preparing the teepee for me, Speaks The Truth, and her two acolytes, Walks Straight Woman and Sees Far Woman.

My instincts were to rush to help, but Speaks the Truth gently restrained me. 'This is their gift to you. It's your time to receive.'

I felt a lump in my throat as I watched these two young women preparing the teepee for me. They did everything with so much grace and care, I could have believed they were setting things out for a lover. Sees Far Woman, discovering my sleeping bag was rather small, asked Speaks The Truth if I could borrow hers, which was a double sleeping bag and much more comfortable than my own. Jamie Sams had told me that I would be sleeping on a down mattress, and, sure enough, it spilled out over the padded layers beneath.

The teepee was about twelve feet in diameter. The bed had been placed at the far wall opposite the entrance. To one side was a small hand basin, to the other my bag containing my journal and other essentials. In the centre was a fire pit with a grid over it, on which I could boil water. And to one side of the fire pit the women had placed an altar, exquisitively arranged with a drum, a rattle, feathers, sage grass, candles and other sacred objects. Each item had been carefully chosen for its symbolism or healing properties.

A small table had been placed on the opposite side of the teepee and on this the women had placed the Sacred Path Cards, the Medicine Cards, and the Lakota Sweat Lodge Cards. These were to help me link the personal to the universal, to understand better the symbolic milestones on the sacred journey of life, and this particular personal challenge. A great concession to modernity was a portable toilet. In traditional quests, I had been told, all functions of the body had to be dealt with within the confines of the circle in which the aspirant spent the four days and nights. A hole was dug when needed to take body waste, and covered up afterwards. The humility such acts engendered was accounted for in my own case by having to place the toilet outside my circle every day for it to be emptied by one of my helpers.

Speaks The Truth called me aside and explained what was to happen. She pointed to a broken circle of stones, outside at the back of the teepee. 'That's a medicine wheel which you'll need to restore, as it'll be your sacred circle. What I suggest is that you continue a line of stones, either side of the entrance, in the east, to connect with the fireplace in front of the teepee. That way, you'll have an enclosed area, with the teepee in the centre, in which you'll have to remain for the next four days and nights. You'll need to collect rocks and firewood, so I suggest you use this as your medicine walk, and when you're ready you can go inside and remain there. Once inside your sacred space, you'll find you're in a different world.' She told me that I would be brought soup every evening, and that there would be fruit and cereal, and very light snacks which I could eat, if I wanted, at any other time of the day. There would also be tea or other drinks, which I could make in the teepee.

'I suggest you start by making thirteen tobacco ties to represent the thirteen original clan mothers, alongside any prayer ties you want to make to the four directions, and to Mother Earth, Grandfather Sky, and Great Spirit, or Great Mystery.'

When they had prepared the teepee for me, the others gave me a hug and wished me well before leaving me to my own devices, saying that one or other would look in on me later that day to make sure everything was all right. After they had gone, I set off among the cactus, ponderosa and pinyon trees to find rocks for the medicine wheel, and wood for the fire. Normally, the medicine walk would take a full day's sojourn in the wilderness, where one would watch for animals, or any other aspects of nature, for what they might teach one. In my case, I had not only experienced the four days in the desert, during which I had done my medicine walk, but the whole of the time I had been travelling in New Mexico had been a medicine journey. It had been a wilderness to me when I arrived, and I had travelled alone, with little security, to face whatever challenges or learnings might come my way. I had encountered many of life's teachers, the weather and the terrain, loneliness, and uncertainty. The whole time had been a preparation for this quest. I did not want to delay any longer. I was impatient to seclude myself in the stillness and the silence. I did not linger collecting the rocks and wood, but completed my tasks as quickly as possible and withdrew into my refuge.

As advised, I had placed a tiny amount of tobacco, that revered plant, at each of the rocks that symbolized the four directions, and at the centre stone, the place of spirit, as an offering to show my gratitude for the opportunity to be in this special healing place. I sprinkled tobacco around the circle, remembering that this represented the sacred hoop within which all life is maintained, and I said a special word of thanks as I closed the final gap between myself and the world. As I put the last rock in place, I breathed a sigh of relief. I had waited a long time to do this ceremony, which I knew was important for me. In the search to find the right place to do it, I had met many wonderful people and experienced many special events. I was deeply grateful at the way I had been guided from one stage to the next, and from one special person to another. I had been safe and cared for at every step of the way.

Once in the tent, I lit the sage that the women had left for me and smudged myself. As I wafted the smoke all around me, I consciously let go of my connection to the world outside, and to the past which had brought me here. I picked up the beautifully decorated feather fan that had been placed on the altar, and began to smudge everything in the tent. This act of purification was also a blessing, and when I had finished inside the teepee, I took the smouldering sage outside, in the abalone shell provided, and wafted the aromatic smoke all around the enclosed area. With this done, I had sealed and purified my space, and made it sacred. I would not step beyond the border of this confined area for another four days and nights. To all intents and purposes I had moved beyond normal time and space. I was in unknown territory and would continue to journey throughout this period of isolation, but the journey would be inwards to the place of vision.

I had been warned not to have expectations of what I might experience during my retreat. Vision, I was told, came in many ways, as feelings or insights, dreams or healing, and not everyone saw some unearthly spectacle. On the strength of my recent visitation from the three black cats, I firmly hoped for some inspirational dream or insight rather than some strange spectre that might put me to flight. 'Trust that you'll get what you need,' I had been advised so many times, 'even if what you need is different from what you want. Spirit knows best what's right for you.'

I put a cushion on the ground outside the teepee entrance and sat in the sun tearing up strips of cloth to make the prescribed prayer ties. I could not remember the names of the thirteen original clan mothers and had to refer to Jamie Sams's book for this and the qualities of each different spiritual archetype. I made several squares out of each coloured cloth, estimating that I would probably make more tobacco ties as time went on. It seemed to take an age to make all the ties to the clan mothers, but when I had finished I felt I had done a good job of invoking their presence and I decided to hang them in the teepee over my bed. They made a colourful bit of bunting, however miniature.

I had a rest, soaking up the sunshine, before going to the medicine wheel to make the prayer ties, in keeping with its tradition. I was aware as I entered that this was hallowed ground where someone before me had called in the different spirits. I had to ask permission to enter. There emerged nothing untoward to deter me from going in. To begin with, I sat near the centre rock and reminded myself of the magic and mystery that had inspired the creation of the first medicine wheel as a place to strengthen one's connection to nature and the whole of the universe, and to know one's place and purpose in the vast scheme of things. Medicine wheels had first appeared as long ago as 50,000 years or more. They were initially built where the earth's energy could be strongly felt. Anyone can build these sacred circles, in their own homes or gardens, or even in the wilderness; but wherever they are built, their use in ceremony empowers the place, making it sacred.

As I had been taught, I invoked the spirit of each direction, asking that I might be blessed with the wisdom that each embodied. I asked for a healing on every level of my being, and that I might gain some insight on my role from hereon. I expressed my gratitude for all that I had received so far on my journey, and for the wonderful women who were supporting this quest of mine. I thought about Wally and Kari, and prayed for their wellbeing and happiness. When that was done, I sat and let the import of the ceremony wash over me. After a while of sitting with soft focus, and listening with some detachment to the idle chatter of nearby birds, my mind detached itself from its moorings and slowly took wing, soaring ever higher, like an eagle, towards the distant mountains. For a time immeasurable, I coasted along the pathways of my life.

I thought about my childhood after my adoption, first in Cambridge where I lived for a couple of years with my new family, and then in Sri Lanka, with schooling in south India for part of that time, until I was eighteen. Our house in Colombo, where I stayed with my parents and four of my brothers, abutted a street where cyclists and pedestrians ran the gauntlet of rickshaws, cars and lorries. Boutiques lined the opposite side of the road, their garishly coloured bottled drinks brighter even than the colourful sarees of their customers. Day and night, above the hawking of men chewing betel juice, and the clamour of voices shouting and laughing, I would hear the timpani of a metal bottle-opener clanking along a line of bottled mineral water. Over and over again, for hours on end, throughout the day and night the makeshift 'xylophone' played the same tune.

I'd gaze out through the barred windows of my bedroom at the street drama: the beggars, some of them maimed, dragging themselves along the dirt on their haunches; dogs running around yapping; men drinking and smoking or making little parcels out of betel leaves lined with white 'lime' paste in which they would wrap some betel nut. The road was spattered with the red juice they spat out. The heavy perfumes of frangipani, which we called the 'temple tree', gardenia, and jacaranda mingled with the spices and garlic coming from the stalls over the road, where food was regularly prepared. Blaring music from radios and gramophones added to the heady cocktail of sights and sounds. Occasionally, drums would be heard from somewhere in the near distance, 'drumming to cast out evil spirits from someone sick'.

Without my realizing it, the exposure to other people's beliefs and customs, both in Sri Lanka and India, seeded an acceptance of aspects of spirituality which a more provincial upbringing might have rejected. Buddhism's belief that we return again and again to tread the wheel of life until we reach a state of enlightened detachment, together with Hindu esoteric teachings about reincarnation and the journey of the soul, and the nature of the etheric forces that underpin all life and reality, added to the store of universal wisdom that my teachers began to expound during my awakening. This same universal wisdom is hidden among much of the Native American's spiritual tradition and thankfully is being shared by some of its medicine people.

Through people such as Joseph Rael, Jamie Sams, Grandmother Twylah and Crowhawk whom I felt blessed to have known, the universal truths are being spread. The medicine people I knew were not encouraging people to 'become Indian' but rather to develop one's highest potential.

Those years in London, after returning from the East, had seemed bleak and lonely after the companionship and colour of the life I had led. But drama school brought a friend with whom I shared a flat throughout college. And all these years on, Pauline and her husband John are still close family friends, and godparents to my first child, Kari. Their home had been a base for our family for years when we came back from our travels. I could still see a picture of Kari, a curly-headed brunette aged four, newly back from Greenland where she had been taught a healthy respect for dogs, uttering a blood-curdling command used by the Inuit to keep the huskies away. Pauline's young retriever had shot under the kitchen table, never to appear when Kari was near.

Then I recalled John speaking at Pascale's memorial service. He talked about an evening a few months before when Pascale was staying at their house. While they were sitting in the garden in the early evening, they heard two owls call. He had not heard or seen them again until the night Pascale died, when they reappeared near where John and Pascale had been sitting. Owl is the symbol for wisdom because it sees what others cannot see. Since she was a small child, Pascale had been able to see people, and to know their worth. I had a sense that this perception had deepened into an appreciation of things that needed changing in the world, and was touched by the efforts she made to do her bit.

I found 'A Profile of Myself' which she had written soon after her fifteenth birthday for a school project. Certain things I still recalled:

NAME:	Pascale Herbert
AGE:	5,370 days, or 177 months and 15 days, or 7,732,800 minutes
DATE OF BIRTH:	30 March, 1978
PLACE OF BIRTH:	Leamington Spa
HAIR:	Long, brown/ginger, wavy
EYE COLOUR:	Green, slightly hazel-coloured
ANIMALS:	One black labrador called Thule
INTERESTS:	Drama, social issues, children
FAVOURITE MUSIC:	Jazz, blues, and a lot of pop
WHAT I HATE:	Animal cruelty, war, poverty, homelessness, and other social issues
WHAT I DO IN MY SPARE TIME:	Go out with my friends, go shopping and swimming, do my homework, go petitioning and leafleting
FAVOURITE ANIMAL:	I absolutely love dolphins (and whales)

WHAT I WANT TO DO WHEN I AM OLDER:	I would like to work with Greenpeace, or I would like to work with children, or I would like to work with dolphins, or I would like to work in the media (drama)
OTHER ISSUES:	I want to get on with my career before getting married. Also I don't want to have a child of my own, I want to adopt a child as there are too many without homes in Romania. I hope to get a career where I do all of the things above!

In the last six months of her life how often had I seen her look at me with eyes of ancient wisdom. Her knowledge was light years beyond my own at the same age, tempered by such joy and a sense of fun. As I looked back over the fifteen months since she had died, I knew I had come a long way in my own transformation.

'To hold, one must detach,' the Tibetan master Djwhal Khul said, 'and to keep one must release.' I had known that for years. I remember Krishnamurti, writing about the loss of a twin brother, saying he had been devastated by the loss, and had retreated, given over to the process of mourning for ten days and nights. At the end of this period, he felt all grief had gone and he was united at profound levels with the twin who had died. I had been told by so many spiritual teachers how important it was not to hold Pascale back. 'There is a time for grieving and a time for letting go.'

I had been taught by various healers that, in the three days following death, the soul, or spirit body, or etheric body as some call it, gradually releases its hold on the physical body, to which it has been attached by a silver cord. Normally it takes about three days for that cord to sever. If we try and hold on to the person who has died, it can seriously impair his/her ability to 'lift off' from the material plane. This can be very harmful and painful for the departed soul.

I had been blessed by having as friends Ken and Else, two people well versed in the affairs of the spirit. Else's special gift is to act as a spiritual midwife for the departed soul. In her prayer and meditation, she literally sees their whole process of detachment from the physical. During this time, she protects and nurtures the departing soul, accustoming it to its new surroundings, helping it to move towards the light, helping it to be free. Else and Ken were the first people I called for help. They came around to the house within minutes, and quietly and unobtrusively started their vigil even while the ambulance men and the doctor were still present. That night, Ken slept with us in the house. Else went home on her own. 'Don't worry about Pascale,' she said to me. 'I'll look after her.' What a gift she had given us. We had still to come to terms with the fact of Pascale's death, and with our own grief. I had no energy to look after Pascale at that moment, but so desperately needed to know she was safe.

Once home, Else had phoned another healer friend to put out the alert, so that within minutes a constant flow of healing energy would be sent out to Pascale and ourselves.

Once we knew she and Richard were doing this it helped us enormously in our ability to deal with the tragedy.

'You don't know how much you are loved,' an acquaintance said when I met her in town a couple of weeks later.

'I do,' I replied. 'We can feel it.'

At the memorial service, Pascale's friends had sung her favourite songs. They sat in the altar pews with eyes red-rimmed, looking like a band of forlorn angels. They read some of her poems, and recited others that she would have loved, and one of them, Megan, encapsulated the essence of Pascale in a poem she had written for the occasion.

Pascale

When something or someone goes missing
And all that seems left is a space,
There are things which will always remind you,
Of what you can never replace.
Hearing the voice of Bob Marley
Sing 'Redemption'; her favourite song
Or the playful noises of dolphins
As they swim free, where they belong.

News of a 'circus show' elephant
Being re-released in the wild
Or a beautiful flower coloured purple,
Or the face of a contented child.
From now on whenever we're smiling
A part of our joy is for her
Our friendship was cheerful and special
A feeling that death can't deter.

We somehow feel we've been cheated
Since someone so special has gone
But we know that although we can't see her
Our memories will always live on.
And although in our eyes there are tears
And our faces say we are sad
We will always remember Pascale,
And all the wonderful times that we had.

A couple of weeks later, my friend Richard came over and gave me a 'reading' about the recent events. 'I can tell you that Pascale has landed,' he said. 'She'll be starting a period of rest soon, which she needs. But if you need to contact her in an emergency, she'll be around. You must know that her time was truly up. She had even delayed her going by a few weeks. She could do this because she's a soul of great dimension, and has been a healer in many lifetimes. There was an angelic presence waiting in the room at her death, which caught her as she fell. It happened instantly. There was absolutely no pain. She had accomplished all that she had come to do. Even so, she has her soul journey to continue on other planes, and her work here can best be done from that dimension.'

'When I look at her picture, Richard, I feel such love emanating from it. It gives me such comfort, and a sense of blessing.'

'That's because Pascale channels from the source, and always has done,' explained Richard. 'She's a being of light. She is also your soulmate, and that is why you had such a deep connection, and why you recognized her when she was born. You'll always be together. She wants me to tell you that all she has done is to drop her body.'

I felt comforted by what he had said. I had felt her presence at the start of the reading embodying and surrounding me, enveloping me in a tingling, vibrant cocoon of love.

'As long as the three of you walk the earth, she has promised to be with you,' Richard said. 'And while it's natural and healthy for you to grieve, you must remember that to continue to grieve without consciously releasing her can have a very detrimental effect on her, and be harmful. My suggestion is that you dive into the grief, and move beyond it. You'll then experience Pascale even more deeply than you experienced her here.'

I had taken that counsel to heart and had entered into my forty days' challenge to release Pascale. I had written in my journal on the fifteenth day: 'I feel lighter today. This process of monitoring my thoughts and bringing in the light is an "enlightening" experience. Pascale, little mother, friend, companion, wise woman, beautiful daughter, babe and infinite being, I see your picture and smile back at you. How wise you had grown. With eyes of ancient wisdom you watched my soul grow. My treasure, you were the most fragrant of fragrances, the most beautiful of flowers, the soul of tenderness and compassion – my sweetest love.'

On the eighteenth day, I met Richard again. He said he thought I was on the point of releasing Pascale. The news had made me sad. Did I want to? I drove to the beach engulfed in sobs, feeling such pain and grief. Through to the next day I was overcome by the loss. I could not even get out of bed, I needed its warmth and cossetting so much. Wally had brought in so many little things to try and comfort me: pictures of Pascale, and of Mother Meera, an avatar, the embodiment of the divine feminine. I had an aching remembrance of discovering Pascale and the awful realization that she was dead. It seemed so unbelievably final. Wally came in again with some beautiful flowers and a red rose each for Pascale and for me.

By the twentieth day I was still feeling a bit dead inside, which moved into anger a few days later. What if it had all been a mistake – if there'd been no purpose in it whatsoever? The coroner's court was such an ordeal. I had mentally to lift myself above its awfulness. In my mind's eye, I think of Pascale as if she is Sleeping Beauty during this rest time. When she wakes, she will have been healed of any pain and sorrow and will be in a different level of being. I frequently want to call her, but know that our bond is so close she would rush to my side, and delay her journey, and I could not have that happen. I have a plethora of books by my bed which all talk about life, and death, reincarnation and rebirth. I read in John Randolph Price's *The Angels Within Us*, 'At the core of the Ancient Mystery Schools was the intention to help the initiate "die" to the personality and awaken to the divine reality within. The core of the idea was that the only true death is physical birth, and the only true birth is the realization and freeing of the spiritual Self.'

Yogananda, a mystic and spiritual teacher from India, says, 'The human being is a cluster of the creative thoughts and consciousness of God which physical death cannot destroy.' That's all very well, I think to myself, but he didn't know Pascale, and how beautifully human she was. I had a mental picture of the two of us in the bath as she was growing up, the tenderness and sharing, the battles with wet sponges at times, and the solving of the world's problems at others. I had no problem believing in life after death and the continuance of the spirit, but nothing made up for the lack of hugs or fun we shared. My eyes caught the advice, 'It is unwise and can be dangerous to toy with the spirit world through seances and mediums; you cannot contact saints or loved ones through such channels, but if you are truly sincere, it is possible by meditation and spiritual development to contact departed loved ones.' I felt comfortable with that thought. I did not want to indulge in spiritualism, but I knew that the seers who guided me were at a spiritual level beyond that, in the realms Yogananda had spoken of, and had perception and integrity enough to access realms that were closed to the rest of us.

Yogananda went on to say, 'God does not want us to limit our love to the members of our family, but to learn to give that love to the whole world. It is to teach us this that the members of our family are taken away one by one; thus we learn to love others. But if we love purely and unselfishly and develop spiritually, we can learn the secret science of maintaining our link with our loved ones after death. If you seek a departed loved one, by strongly and continuously meditating on that soul, you will receive an answer.' All our family had been able to contact Pascale when we needed to, but we respected her need to be left alone.

By the twenty-seventh day I commented in my journal that I feared no alchemy was taking place within me. That day I read from *The Angels Within Us*, 'The Angel of Death does not represent the end but the real meaning of death – the gateway to a larger life in reality. This angel represents the force of metamorphosis. That which we call death is but an entrance into a more glorious life of joy, fulfilment, peace and freedom, whether the experience is physical or metaphysical. In each case, it is an unceasing flow of sentient life, but with a difference. Except for the immediate uplift of consciousness derived from the experience of being freed from the corporeal body, physical death is nothing more than a change in form. We maintain the awareness, understanding, and knowledge gained during our visit on earth and carry our tendencies and interests with us as we move from one plane to another.' That made sense to me and reiterated what I had learned from my first mentor and the channelled material that came through him. Something began to heal in my emotions.

The next day had started with my discovering more things of Pascale's which we had either to burn or get rid of. It shakes one up. I felt distant with no real connection to the moment and suffered a dull ache throughout most of the day. The clothes brought me right back to the physicality of the loss. What's life all about? I asked myself again. Why invest so much in love and in family life if it is all going to be taken away? I wrote in my journal, 'How precious it was to watch your development, Pascale. How many laughs we shared together, how many confidences and caresses. As I give away more little things of yours, another level of feelings emerges, my eyes start to prick, I breathe deeply. Wally complains that your room seems so empty, things keep disappearing, and yet we have only got rid of unimportant things, or kept those closest to us that forged a special link.'

I continued in my journal, 'It's good to give some things away that hold a strong attachment, otherwise we might always stay at that needy emotional level and miss out on experiencing you at those levels that can never be lost. There's no separation, I know. Merging is the answer. That's what we have to practise more. I feel a surge of energy today, and yet a need to be mothered myself. I am grateful for all my blessings. Beloved you are, Pascale. I thought about that word, 'beloved' . . . the search for the beloved, isn't that what life's about? We see the beloved in many people but more so in some than others. Some are the beloved incarnate, they channel from the source. That phrase recurs in my mind every time I look at your picture.'

Did a person's death echo our being torn from the beloved – a memory of the original 'Fall' – an echo of the sadness, longing and despair? Pascale seemed to be smiling at me as I wrote this. How strange that every picture taken of Pascale recently was in soft focus! It makes me wonder if in the last six months your spirit was beginning to loosen its connection to the body. By the time the fortieth day had come, I had experienced a gamut of emotions from sorrow, grief and anger, to despair and hopelessness. In the last week of it, Wally and I had talked about our deeply depressed state. At least we could acknowledge it and not shut it off or swallow it. It was so good to be able to share it. It came to me that alongside our grieving for Pascale we had to look at the experience as an unique teaching. Instead of giving up because of what we had lost – and we had lost a great treasure, a comforter, a bringer of joy and hope, innocence, wisdom and compassion – we had to ask what she was making us face.

What has her departure forced us to do? To share, to attune to each other so that we can feel together even when we are miles apart, to search for answers to essential questions, to go deeper into the mystery. And yet all the time Pascale is there, beckoning us on. When I am very still and empty, I feel her presence like a warm glow around me. Things seem to happen with her touch to them. Lots of little things occur which seem to bear her influence – sometimes funny little things, as though she has orchestrated them. We must have courage, have faith, keep going. We are learning so many lessons in mastery – self-mastery – all because of Pascale.

I thought about so much that first afternoon inside the medicine wheel. When had the alchemy happened? There had been a great lightening of my spirits after those forty days; even though I still missed her, something had shifted. What it had done was to concentrate and focus my energy so that I had moved through the processes faster. Here in New Mexico, again, I had gone through another pain barrier, and then, recently, I could not tell the exact moment, something major had cleared in me. I felt a deep healing within.

A clink of metal nearby alerted me to the arrival of Looks Far Woman with a canister of soup. She glided off as silently as she had arrived after a brief look of enquiry. I acknowledged that all was fine and withdrew inside the teepee for my meal. Time had evaded me and it was the end of the afternoon already.

I lit a fire in the teepee and sat idly gazing at the flames as they danced and leaped in the freshening breeze. I had been warned not to have too big a fire or I would be smoked out of the teepee; even so, a cloud billowed up from the tiny conflagration, stinging my eyes and making me cough and seek fresh air. I had put pictures of the family on the altar next to a large turquoise bear fetish which symbolized introspection. The bear represents the west and going within. Its teaching is that we must enter the great void inside ourselves to find the answers we seek.

Beside this, Walks Straight Woman had placed a brightly coloured branch which was painted like a snake. The message of this creature is transmutation. Snake medicine, according to Jamie Sams, is the power of creation, embodying sexuality, psychic energy, alchemy, reproduction, and ascension. Snake medicine people, she says, are very rare. Their special task is to transmute poison, be it mental, physical, spiritual or emotional. I thought of Standing Eagle whose power animal is the snake, and I realized that Walks Straight Woman had put the snake there to remind me of the transformational nature of this ceremony I was doing. It was to remind me to let go of anything I no longer needed, be it feelings or emotions, attitudes, or thought forms, just as a snake sheds its skin before growing a new one. This ceremony was an opportunity to come into balance on every level.

As Speaks The Truth had suggested, I drew five cards from the combined decks of cards to see what their message was to me. In the north I drew the Story-teller, in the east Fire, in the south the Drum, in the west Earth, and in the centre Beaver. I was amazed at their revelation. The Story-teller card spoke of expansion on all levels. It indicated that I was growing and encompassing new ideas, and that I had earned this success. It also went on to say that, through the story-teller sharing her experiences, she helped other people to grow. It encouraged, by suggesting that I was beginning to remember my personal 'medicine' or gifts, and that I was moving more towards my potential.

In the east, the Fire card said that it represented the eternal life, the great power of Wakan Tanka, Great Spirit. It advised me to examine my inner flame, my inner truth, for whatever I spoke or did would be passed on to my children and to other people. In the south, the Drum spoke of rhythm and internal timing. The drum represented the heartbeat of the earth mother, and through it one could not only connect with her rhythm but one could journey to other states of consciousness and parallel universes. It called on me to find my own natural rhythm and to come back into harmony with myself. It advised that I let myself become in tune with Mother Earth's heartbeat, which meant that I should not let my mind outdistance what my body could handle. This struck a deep note in me. My mind often did outpace my body, and as a result I frequently exhausted myself trying to keep up with my ideas.

The west card, too, spoke eloquently. It signified birth, and offered the gift of being creative through one's own individual expression. It went on to say that in the near future I might find myself giving birth to a new idea, or a new enterprise, or starting my life anew in some way. It said that I might already have begun this, and that the way to do it successfully was to embrace the new birth by releasing the images and symbols of the past. Accept the changes that come, it advised. 'You can make the changes you have been wanting to make in your life.' I should, however, take the time to stand on the earth, and let her energy and support invigorate me. Once again, the wisdom of the cards spoke to my heart.

There was one card left, the Beaver, representing the centre and the principle that held the others together. Its message was clear: I was to visualize the goal I wished to accomplish and be willing to work with others to achieve that end. I could handle that. I wrote the messages of each card in my journal and gave thanks for their wisdom. How very appropriate they had all been. I understood better now how our teaching came from such diverse things as the cards, animals, stones, or even clouds. In Native American philosophy they all had spirit in them. In Beautiful Painted Arrow's words they were all metaphors for spiritual principles or ideas. And in Native American tradition, modern physics, and Eastern philosophy, everything is related, everything is connected, everything is a form of energy. And what is the Great Mystery, but the energy that contains and is contained in every single aspect of life.

That evening, before turning in, I took a couple of large cushions into the medicine wheel and placed them near the centre. Lying down on them, I gazed up at the night sky, mesmerized by its celestial diamonds. Somewhere out there were the Pleiades, from which several of the Native tribes claimed their origin. As I lay there, I thought of the medicine wheel and how it represented all the lessons we needed to learn on our journey through life. As we go from childhood, in the south, through life's teachings and reflect on them in the west, we arrive, finally, at the place of wisdom in the north. Our spirits are supposed to leave from here, according to Jamie Sams, and travel around the wheel to the east, the place of enlightenment and of wholeness. This is also the gateway to all other levels of awareness. When we return, it is believed, for another incarnation, we come in through the east gateway, and our spirits travel to the south where they are born into physical bodies once again.

The medicine wheel represents all the cycles of life, planting, gestation, birth, growth, change, death and renewal. We all go through many changes, many little deaths, many opportunities for renewal. Where was I in the scheme of things? Change, movement, it was a time for renewal. An ending of a cycle and, because of that, the beginning of a new one. What would that bring? Perhaps I did not need to know that answer immediately. Perhaps all I needed to do at this stage was to allow myself to be healed, to tie up any loose ends from the past, and be patient and receptive for whatever was approaching me from the future.

The teepee glowed with a warm ambient light from the candles I had lit. It seemed symbolic of safety and protection. I went inside and made myself a hot drink. I had closed the flap but the wings at the top of the teepee were wide open, letting in the night sky. As a result, it was becoming a bit chill inside, but I didn't want to fold them over and exclude the stars. So I decided to clamber into the sleeping bag, to have my drink, and marvelled, delightedly, at how warm and cosy it felt. When I blew out the candles, I was plunged into a velvet, diamond-studded blackness.

Somewhere in the hills nearby a coyote barked. Now, what was that telling me? I asked myself. Everything that impinged on one's consciousness in a vision or healing quest was supposed to be of relevance. What could the trickster, as the coyote was called, teach me? He was the animal for the south. He came to remind one not to take things too seriously, to laugh at oneself and to see the humour in all things. Through laughter, we could often see a different point of view. Was he telling me that I should enjoy myself? I fell asleep remembering Jamie Sams's instruction that I should revel in every step of the journey, every point of the medicine wheel, and it would be delicious.

I must have woken early, although I had no clock to tell the time. I had several times started out of sleep during the night to hear the sharp retort of the teepee flaps being wildly agitated by the wind. Great gusts swept around the teepee, and I had to wrap my head in a shawl, the air was so cold. But, once this was done, the thick sleeping bag and down mattress had kept me warm and snug.

My first task on getting dressed was to light a fire, not only to warm the teepee, but to boil a kettle for tea. I spent the first part of the morning doing some stretching exercises followed by some tai chi. I reflected that I was already into my second day, and still feeling rather wordly. Perhaps visions did not arrive in such circumstances and I would somehow have to become much more introspective.

The drum, when used properly, connects the player or listener to the heartbeat of the earth. It has also been known to induce a state of consciousness that facilitates travel into other dimensions or realities. So, in an effort to transport myself into a state of receptivity, I brought out the beautiful drum Karen had lent me and sat in the sun playing. The rich, vibrant tones soon created a deep and pleasurable resonance within me. I was not carried off into magical realms, but after drumming intently for some time I lost the desire for flights of fancy and became instead gently subdued by its sonorous rhythm. I was reminded of the card I had picked out the previous evening with its message that I should find my proper rhythm, and not let my overactive mind run away with me.

Much of the afternoon was taken up making more tobacco ties in deep contemplation, focusing on my intention as I crafted each one. Then, later that evening I found myself bursting into song without consciously willing it. And every time, I found myself singing the words of that wonderful hymn, 'Amazing Grace, how sweet the sound, that saved a wretch like me. I once was lost, but now am found, was blind but now I see.' This was to happen several times during the next two days. I would go through a gamut of emotions and feelings, and then these would pass and I would burst into song again!

I was woken and then serenaded over my morning tea on the third day by the joyful and ecstatic song of a small bird. I tried responding in kind but even my best warble was a poor substitute for its glorious paean. The day was colder than previously. Speaks

The Truth brought out a hot bagel for my breakfast. It was a lovely gesture, and she satisfied herself that all was well with me. I was pleased to discover I did not need to eat much, but I did need lots of hot drinks. Feeling quite active but peaceful, I decided to get my bedding out to air when the sun became warmer. I performed my tai chi exercises with great attention. I felt an extraordinary desire to tidy my area and went all over it, picking up the small stones and twigs that I had barely noticed before.

As the day wore on, I seemed to be in two worlds, an inner reflective state, and an outer perceptive one. From the medicine wheel, looking west, the far mountains rose beyond a sea of green splashed with pink adobe. The beige sparseness of the nearest mountain range contrasted with the grey-blue of the mountains beyond, which were streaked with snow. There was something compelling about the scene. I had an urge to meld with the mountains and become one with them and yet to remain separate enough to see their beauty. I was reminded of just how beautiful was this planet. But how easy it is to lose our connection to our earth mother. I could see the little coloured parcels, my tobacco ties, lying in a circle, reminders of my intention to become more aware.

By mid-afternoon, the ease of the morning had vanished. Restlessness had got me by the throat and I was at screaming pitch. I felt disconnected and disenchanted. I stomped around the teepee complaining loudly of my boredom. I wanted to yell at the world and tell it how excruciatingly dull it had become. One minute I was angry, the next miserable. Like a whirlwind that appears out of the blue, my thoughts and emotions swept down on my sense of security and scattered it to the four directions. Voices of doubt and fear bombarded me with a host of accusations that were totally undermining. They carped and chided me, telling me that I was fooling myself if I thought anything significant was happening. I strode around the teepee to try and get away from them, but they continued to tug and tear at my sense of trust. Any feeling of wellbeing vanished.

I must have struggled for several hours with the battalion of demons that assailed me. 'You're bored. Give up! You are only wasting your time. There's no alchemy here. It only works for the Native people.' I sat in the centre of the medicine wheel feeling desolate. Maybe I was fooling myself with this whole concept of vision questing. Maybe there was no such thing as a rite of passage. Maybe I had not grown at all. Maybe this was all a self-indulgence. Maybe . . . maybe . . . maybe. I sat hugging my knees, my head buried on them. I felt drained of emotion, empty, all hope and expectations gone. And in that moment of emptiness and detachment something happened.

In my mind's eye, I was standing on a hill overlooking a herd of buffalo. As I saw the buffalo, I felt a great opening of my heart. A sense of love and compassion spread outwards from me, together with a sorrow that they had nearly all been lost. At the same moment, I felt a tremor in the ground beneath me as if shaken by passing hooves. The air around me palpitated with what seemed a great and wonderful presence, and I found myself bathed in a fleeting euphoric glow. In almost a dream state, I looked towards a couple of birds hovering high in the sky. They wheeled and glided in slow and measured curves. They were joined by another, and then another two. All five moved in concert. Were they hawks, or ravens, or crows? Hawk was a messenger. It signified a challenge conquered, a lesson completed, the cleansing of emotion that clouded vision. Could hawk be speaking to me? Had I really passed the test? Was it telling me, on all five cardinal points of the medicine wheel, that I had, in fact, come through my rite of passage?

What if it were raven, the carrier of magic, the messenger of the void? Raven signifies the approach of a change in consciousness. Raven is the guardian of ceremonial magic and absent healing. Raven can be the carrier of one's messages to spirit; it could also mean that spirit might be calling you. Was raven calling to me, or was it crow? Crow had appeared to me in the cards before. Crow, the keeper of sacred law, the shape-shifter, the one who bends physical laws – was crow calling to me? If crow called, it too was an omen of change. It called one to honour the higher spiritual order above that created by human culture. It called one to speak one's truth and to follow one's life mission.

As I sat, musing over the significance of the different omens, there was a commotion to my right. In a flurry of feathers and flapping wings, a single crow took flight pursued by four others, from were they had alighted moments before on a nearby tree. I had been so busy trying to decipher the nature of the birds I had been watching that I had not seen them swoop down from the now empty space in the sky. There was the answer plain as day. The crow was to be my guide – alongside the buffalo – and I had seen five of them to prove the point. I smiled to myself. The humble crow – who'd have thought this master of disguise would appear as my mentor? A part of me had hoped it would be a hawk or raven that would favour me as a companion – they seemed more glamorous for some reason. But crow was good enough. Crow knew about magic and mystery. I was ready to accept crow and the privileges and learning that this liaison would bring. When I got up from my daydreaming, I had an irresistible urge to dance and dance, and dance. I had completed countless turns of the medicine wheel before my elation would allow me to stop. The western horizon was shot with great streaks of fire that vanished into the depths of indigo and purple. Looks Far Woman approached with some corn bread and a canister of soup. She looked enquiringly at me and smiled as if she knew what I had experienced. I could have jumped over the boundary and hugged her. I have done what I came to do, I wanted to shout. I don't need to stay any longer! I have done it! I have really done it! I can come out now! I stifled my urge to talk to her. I could only bow in acknowledgement of my gratitude to her.

That evening I built a huge fire in front of the teepee. The wind sent the flames high in jagged holly-leaved shapes. It flared and danced wildly and excitingly. Sparks flew off it into the night, and darted and leaped into the shadows. I could imagine they were fireflies bobbing about, appearing and disappearing again. I sat up late, enjoying the fire's company, feeling a great sense of peace and tranquillity, and feeling of security as if I were in the womb of the world.

I spent a good part of the morning packing up my belongings and tidying up the teepee. Today I was definitely coming out of my introspective mode and kept looking beyond the circle, as if in readiness to step out. But it was late afternoon, when sitting in the teepee and passing the time with some singing, that I heard myself being echoed outside. Speaks The Truth beckoned to me, with her finger over her mouth. She led me back to her house and up to her room, where she gave me a long robe and pointed to the shower. I was to wash and put the robe on in readiness for the final act of the ceremony, the sweat lodge. As I entered the house, several of the women smiled. They had gathered, I was to learn, to welcome me back to the world of normality, and to celebrate my completion of the ritual. It felt wonderful to shower and to be back in the world of people, especially such friendly, caring people.

It was dark by the time the sweat lodge started. About eight of us huddled in our flimsy attire around the fire. I was greeted by smiles and hugs, still in silence. Once inside, Speaks The Truth asked each of us to give our name and our reason for being there. Apart from any personal intention, each of the women said she was there to honour and support me and celebrate the completion of my quest. I was misty-eyed by the time they had all spoken, and felt deeply humbled by what they had said. I had not words enough to speak my gratitude. I introduced myself as Sunlight Through The Trees, and how good it felt to say that. 'Ho!' the others answered in acknowledgement. The bud of sisterhood opened fully as the ceremony got under way.

When it came to my turn to speak, I said I was there to let go of the past, with gratitude for what it had taught and brought to me. Speaks The Truth invited me to share what had gone on during my healing quest. I told them about my moments of boredom and how they had led to moments of enlightenment. I told them I had learned not to let my mind run away, with my body lagging behind it. And that I truly knew something was being born to me, and that I would be happy to know its character when it happened.

When all had spoken, Speaks The Truth asked the two women who had physically supported me to share what the four days had meant to them.

Looks Far Woman looked at me. 'I felt I was journeying with you all the time. I could feel your sadness and your joy. I wanted to dance with you. And one day when I went into the mountains with a friend I felt we'd taken you with us. And then one moment I thought about you so much, and I found myself singing "Amazing Grace".'

'I too travelled with you on your journey,' said Walks Straight Woman. 'And I knew everything was all right. I had a dream that there was a great flowering for you, and that you and Pascale became one.'

There was laughter and pathos in the rest of the sharing and a great bonding established between us all. We ended the sweat lodge by singing a couple of songs which Jamie Sams had written, to the accompaniment of the drum. Before I left the lodge, Speaks The Truth told me to go and shower and then to go to one of the rooms where we would all gather before she gave me a massage.

As I waited in the room indicated, the rest of the women came in. The reason for their presence puzzled me until, one by one, they came over to hand me some beautiful little gift. A piece of turquoise, some little obsidian stones called apache tears, a pair of silver earrings in the shape of a feather, a pink quartz crystal pendant, a carved frog and pussycat, a miniature carved seal, a tiny white buffalo, an elk's tooth were all given to me. Speaks The Truth handed me a beautiful white chamois leather pouch, decorated with beads and a hawk's feather, which she and Looks Far Woman had made specially for me. 'This medicine pouch is for you to carry your personal medicine in, your symbols of power and protection.' I was overcome with joy, surprise, and gratitude at such generosity and friendship. Looks Far Woman handed me the bronze plate she had left for me in the teepee. 'It's a healing plate,' she confided. 'It mirrors your true self.' When I thought there could be no more, another woman came up and handed me a bundle of sage she had gathered at the desert retreat. 'I picked this specially for you,' she said.

Hardly able to speak by this time, I finally managed to express my thanks. We were to share a meal together, but before this Speaks The Truth gave me a wonderful, nurturing massage.

Taught in the Kahuna way, a Hawaiian healing art, the broad nourishing strokes were accompanied by dramatic exhalation of breath, as the healing energy was kneaded into the muscles, with unconditional love. Lynn, a woman with a great sense of humour who, like the others, had become a good friend, massaged my head and then my feet, the two of them transporting my mind and body into a state of bliss. I was still in this wonderfully relaxed and peaceful state when I went downstairs to eat with the others.

I had my own gifts to give those who had served me over the last four days. I gave a brooch to Walks Straight Woman, an antler and crystal talking stick to Speaks The Truth. For Looks Far Woman, who had performed every act of service with such grace and humour, I gave a special memento I had of Pascale, with a little turquoise crescent moon to go with it. It matched a similar crescent moon I had been given by Talks With Bears, which he had said shamans carried in their medicine pouches. As I said goodbye to each of the women who had come to celebrate my healing quest with me, I knew a kinship had been born that would last forever, over the longest time or distance.

CHAPTER FIFTEEN

Emergence

M Y QUEST WAS OVER, BUT THERE WAS STILL ONE TASK
left to me before I could go home, and that was to
return the car to Colorado (I had not bought it,
partly for insurance reasons). The journey to my friends Al and
Hanna, who had found me the vehicle, would take seven to eight
hours, much of it through desolate high altitude. I had travelled
through a good part of it with a friend Donna, a few days before
my retreat. In a wonderful journey which had taken us into a
magical valley at the base of the Rocky Mountains, and on to
Colorado Springs, we had returned via the Great Sand Dunes, an
aptly named geographical curiosity in the midst of mesa and
mountain, and had come, unexpectedly, upon a herd of buffalo.

'What a wonderful symbol for your vision quest,' Donna had
commented. I little dreamed that this same symbol would emerge
during my quest, nor did I know then that it was a reminder to be
grateful for the bounty of the earth, and a symbol of renewal. It
was to remind me also of the vastness of the inner self, of the
power of prayer, and the need to give praise and thanks for prayers
answered. White Buffalo Calf Woman brought the pipe to the
people and taught them how to use it in a sacred manner, as an
instrument of prayer. She had told the people that when they
prayed with it 'they prayed for and with everything'. I was being
reminded also that any gift one is given is to be shared so that
others might benefit from its use.

As I drove the 300 and more miles back to Al and Hanna's I
was reminded of how much I had to be grateful for.

When the time had come to say goodbye to Karen, I had felt sad to be leaving her. 'I can't thank you enough for your generosity and kindness. You've been so wonderfully supportive, I couldn't –'

She interrupted my protestations of thanks. 'It's been a gift for me to have you stay with me!'

We hugged each other. There is an alchemy that happens at times between people when giving and receiving become indivisible. If I mirrored her open-heartedness in any way, it was fair exchange.

So many people had helped and befriended me on my travels. Without this support, my trip could have been an ordeal instead of a journey of discovery. I had been frightened of stepping in the unknown, especially after Kari had left, but my vulnerability had paid off by forcing me to be without masks or armour, to speak and act straight from my heart, and people had responded with heart. The focus of my journey had changed from a quest for vision – with regard to my future work and purpose – to a quest for healing, as the one could only happen after the other. The greatest healing had been the kindness and concern of strangers. In the wake of Pascale's death I had felt stripped of the certainties that guided my life, and did not know what to expect. The structures that held my daily existence together were gone.

Maybe it was because of those insecurities that I felt an urge to travel – not aimlessly without direction, but particularly to be with Native American medicine people. I believed they could help me through this rite of passage, could heal my scattered being, and connect me to those influences that shaped my destiny, so that I could understand and accept the change of circumstances that had come to me, and transform the tragedy into the gifting of a new consciousness, a new state of awareness, that all such initiations carry with them. When I had started my journey, alone, I had felt desolate. On several occasions I had howled my misery and loneliness to the world, purging that bit more the emotions which one has to leave behind if one is to travel with safety into other reaches of the mind, other areas of the psyche, the realms of archetypal visioning and dreaming.

In the early stages, the barren landscape accentuated my feelings of emptiness but, as time wore on, the beauty of the same landscape inspired and honed me. Encouraged to see the world as holy and inseparable from me, invited to participate in ceremony of a sacred and healing nature, I found my quest restoring my love for the world, and my faith in human nature. I had been reminded several times, by different healers, that I could reach Pascale on another level, in another dimension, by clearing my emotions and journeying inwardly to that place of lightness. Through my relationship with Pascale I had been shown a model for how we can all relate when we have a fully opened heart. I could not have loved her more, nor could I have been more loved by her. And this I believe is the potential manner in which we can all relate to each other. The energy of the open heart is that of the self, which is that of spirit. It is channelled directly from the source, and is of the source, expressing the same divine qualities. The experience was something that could never be lost. As I sought to merge with the mountainous grandeur of New Mexico's high desert, I had been shriven by its harsh beauty. From the medicine people and shamans I had met I had been reminded, also, that there is magic at the heart of things, which is available to all of us when we remember our connectedness to all that is and function from this place of consciousness. It was not long before my joy returned and I could trust again.

The kernel of the medicine teachings had been exemplified by certain Native American elders whose philosophy and way of life, inseparable from the spiritual, had confirmed the sacredness in all form, and beyond form. They had reminded me of my connection to Great Mystery, the source, which I still like to think of as Great Spirit, and of the unbreakable web that binds everything in the universe together. They taught me that everything in nature was both my relative and my teacher. And that when one took anything from nature one should ask permission first, and leave an offering, or say a prayer of thanks. They reminded me that the whole of life was held within the sacred hoop, and that all life was equal; that it was my duty to fulfil my potential, knowing that my purpose was to use my gifts for the benefit of all my relations, which included every kingdom of nature, and that of spirit.

I had achieved my rite of passage. I could look back at the past, with all its challenges, joys, and recent sadness, and see it in context, with all its learnings and giftings. I was at peace with myself and with what life had brought me. I had truly released Pascale but could still talk to her and be with her, in a different way. I was not yet totally through the door she had opened for me, but I had engaged with a process on this quest that would take me through it when I was ready for the experience and for the responsibility that would come with it. My heart had been stretched to the extent that I seemed able to love more freely. I could look at youngsters and see Pascale in them, and love them for it, knowing that what I was seeing in them was a reflection of the self, that spiritual essence which we all have in common and which she radiated.

I could face the future, and its mystery, with the excitement and knowledge that a new focus and purpose would inexorably unfold. I had come of age, in Native American terms, and with this came inevitable duties. After the family-orientated role of parent has ended, the role of elder emerges, and with this a broader vision and a responsibility to do one's bit to maintain the balance and harmony of our world. I had been initiated, through Beautiful Painted Arrow, to a level of consciousness whose influence I was yet to become aware of, but which would, inevitably, colour my future work. The message from the different medicine people suggested that Pascale had freed us to go deeper into the Great Mystery, and that she would overlight this.

I thought of this and much more as I drove through the forest near Taos on my last day in New Mexico. I passed barely a soul for mile upon mile through dense woodland, and beyond into alpine meadow, and still further on, through vast open spaces. Had I not travelled some of the route before I would have imagined that the wilderness would never end. Hanna had told me, when she phoned towards the end of February, that I would have to leave Santa Fe within the next couple of days if I wanted to get to them in Evergreen before the big snowfalls that had been forecast. This meant leaving earlier than I intended as I did not want to be caught out in heavy snow. Even with this early start, I could not avoid the bad weather, which swept in ahead of time, creating havoc on the roads. At the wayside café where I stopped for a break after a couple of hours' drive, I overheard lorry drivers complaining about the conditions in Colorado. Denver was impassable, they told me, and warned me not to continue unless I had to. I had avoided driving in heavy snow throughout my time in New Mexico as the car was simply not suited to this type of travel. Today, however, I felt as if nothing would stop me. I had a strong sense of Pascale's presence and felt totally safe and confident about driving on.

Traffic was heavy towards the afternoon, and I was weary by the time I reached Colorado Springs, a huge, sprawling, and busy metropolis, in the early afternoon. Cars lay abandoned by the roadside, an indication of the severity of the conditions earlier in the day. Although the motorway was now reasonably clear, slush spurted over the windows with each passing car.

Traffic continued to build up towards the end of my journey. I had been on the road now for seven hours and I was feeling tired. Distances always seem to expand when one is flagging, and I was beginning to worry that I had taken the wrong turning off the motorway when I saw the sign ahead for Evergreen. As the route became more familiar, I found myself feeling excited. My journey was nearly over, my quest was finished. I would soon be relaxing with friends and it would not be long before I would be going home.

It was almost four o'clock in the afternoon when I pulled up outside my friends' home.

The days following were filled with simple enjoyments. I was indulged in all kinds of treats to make up for any deprivation I might have suffered on my journey. At the end of one particularly wonderful day in the mountains, we returned past a herd of wild elk. I had hoped we would see these majestic creatures before I left. Elk symbolized stamina, according to Native American tradition. I thought back to how my own stamina had stood up to my quest.

One of the revelations on this journey was that things could happen easily, if I followed my instincts, and went with the flow. I had thought a quest had to be physically tough and even frightening for it to be worthwhile, and I had been shown that there was another, gentler, and more nourishing way to achieve the desired results.

In choosing the healing quest, I had been encouraged to strengthen my connection with the earth, the greatest healer, which had been discouraged in my childhood. This connection with the earth is something everyone needs. By connecting with the earth we ground our ideas, we activate them, we heal ourselves, and at the same time we gain access to the wisdom of the universe. The earth is the storehouse of knowledge, according to the medicine people, which we can channel when we attune ourselves to her vibration. The earth, according to the shamans, also magnetizes our electro-magnetic energy, and her energy vitalizes us. We can harmonize with her by listening to the drum, which represents her heartbeat, or through quieting ourselves in nature.

I was reminded also that in this approaching new world, the Fifth World, in which universal peace and harmony is the hallmark, we can all have a part in its creation simply by transforming any conflict or negativity we hold within ourselves. When we are willing to do this, and commit ourselves to the intent, unseen powers come to help and guide us. There are those among the Native Americans and other indigenous peoples in the world, who have, through their own efforts, prayers and ceremonies, sought to preserve and maintain the structure and balance of those elements that keep our world together in harmony. These people have been put in the role of guardians of ancient wisdom, and caretakers of the planet. This is a role they have honoured and fulfilled for untold generations. Now, with the coming of the new millennium, we are asked to take on this responsibility for ourselves. Our fate, and the fate of our planet is in our hands.

With the emergence of this new world comes the opportunity to open our consciousness to other realities, to parallel universes. Already the shamans, the medicine people, the seers and prophets have bridged these worlds. Now, with the awakening of the new consciousness, these other realms are open for each of us to reach and explore. The way each of us can develop our gifts, and fulfil our potential, is to walk the Beauty Path. The Beauty Path, the Native Americans say, is also the path of the heart, the path of right relationships. It is the path we walk when we remember and honour our place in the sacred hoop. It is the path we walk when we honour all kingdoms of nature, and those of spirit, giving equal respect to all life, and seeing all things, all events, all people, as our teachers. It is the path we walk when we seek to express peace and harmony, and tolerance, alongside unconditional love.

Moment to moment, there is the opportunity for each of us to renew ourselves. The vision quest, or healing quest, is a microcosm of that greater initiation, life, which can bring us the vision and the purpose we need when we remember to treat each action as sacred, each person, animal, tree or flower as a metaphor for a much greater spiritual principle or idea. When we remember to treat life as sacred, and every aspect of it with love and respect, we do walk the Beauty Path, which leads to the heart of the Great Mystery.

As I flew home, my excitement at the thought of seeing the family again was balanced by a sense of profound gratitude for the keepers of the sacred wisdom who had inspired and guided my healing quest. The vision that I had been shown, throughout my journey, was of a world to be, reflecting its primal harmony, the sacred hoop renewed. The healing was of my scattered self restored to a greater sense of wholeness. Out of that came a will to serve the promised golden future with whatever might be my newly awakened gifts, and these would unfold at the right time. I had a medicine name to help me remember my quest, and my connection to the world of nature: laughter spills out of me every time I see or think of Sunlight Through The Trees.

Finally, I had been shown how the medicine wheel, that sacred symbol of wholeness and unity, had been gifted to us all, irrespective of race or creed or colour, for us to learn where we stand in relationship to each other, and to the cosmos, or Great Mystery. With the medicine wheel as a model, we can relate our individual growth and change to the universal cycles of birth, death and renewal. We are reminded to see our life as a journey of unfolding potential. We do not need to have learned about the medicine wheel to be part of it, however: all any of us need to remember is that we are connected to each other, and to all that is, by virtue of being within the sacred hoop of life. If ever we feel unable to move on, in any area of our life, we need just to confirm our willingness to grow, and to ask for the help that is always there, waiting for our readiness to commit to the next stage of our unfoldment. At each section of the medicine wheel there are achetypal beings waiting to assist us. Some may see these as the thirteen original clan mothers, others may see these as angels or archangels, and still others may see them as spirits of the different directions, or even daimons, devas, or other guiding principles.

The message that the medicine people everywhere wish to pass on is the sacredness of the world we live in. This world of nature is not, they protest, an inanimate cornucopia of material resources to be plundered at will. Rather is it a dynamic web of interrelating natural forces, imbued with spirit, which the Ancients knew required an elusive but positive exchange of energy to keep renewed and in balance. The natural world, having a vibral core (like ourselves) that contains Great Mystery, as well as being contained by Great Mystery, responds to praise and prayer, love and gratitude. We are called upon to honour and respect our Mother Earth and all the kingdoms of nature; to maintain the balance and harmony of our world, through right relationship with all our relations, that it may be safeguarded down to the seventh generation.

I would never forget what I had learned from Beautiful Painted Arrow, that everything in life is a metaphor for a greater spiritual principle. And that everything that happens to us can be a metaphor for a spiritual learning. I discovered that what best describes the Native people I met is their willingness to sacrifice themselves in order that the people may live. I looked forward to the new world, so eloquently spoken of in their prophecies. In keeping with my vision of the buffalo, 'the symbol of the universe and the vast totality of things', I offered them my deepest gratitude and respect.

Finally, I remembered that wherever we place our consciousness influences how we are, and how we operate in our world. We need to be aware of what it is we identify with, remembering that it controls us and determines our existence. If we identify with limited visions of ourselves, we will live limited lives. If we identify with any one particular aspect of ourselves to the exclusion of the rest, we jeopardize our chances of happiness, or of living a reasonably full and fulfilling life. The secret to empowering oneself is to identify with the self, which has been described as a centre of pure radiance. It is the self that is the perfect model for human potential. At each stage of our development we have to relinquish our attachment to the past and to the roles we have played. Attachments bind us, and stop us from experiencing our wholeness. I learned that each phase of our lives brings with it gifts and talents. No less so the phase of 'elderhood' which is available to us when we come of age. The way to reach these gifts is through the receptive, creative, spiritual, and feminine aspect of our natures, whether we are men or women.

Through the intention and the willingness to open up to our greater potential we activate those channels that bring us the means of doing so. And all we ever need to ask for from Great Spirit, or from whatever transcendant being is closest to our heart, is to reveal 'the next step'.

In completing my rite of passage I had opened up a finer, more intuitive side of my nature which emerged, as Beautiful Painted Arrow had predicted, a few months after his initiation. I also began to use vocal sound again as a tool for healing and self-expression, inspired by the wisdom he had said was inherent in this form of expression. Through sounding, I found I could restore a sense of harmony and balance for myself and for other people. But the most important gift of all that I brought back with me was a deeper sense of who I am, and a groundedness that spoke of my new relationship with the earth, and a joyful sense of renewed purpose. In being among the Native American medicine people, and practising ceremony with them, I had redeemed a lost part of my psyche, a part that responds to ritual and chant, to mystery and spirit. Sometimes our uniqueness is hidden in these lost parts of ourselves. And unless we find these parts, we cannot realize their qualities. The qualities I had touched through journeying among the Native people had all to do with opening the heart.

In acknowledgement of all I have learned, I salute all my relations – Mitakuye Oyasin! May you all walk in harmony with yourselves and with each other and with Great Mystery. Ho!

RESOURCES

TO EVERYBODY WHO READS THIS BOOK I WOULD SAY THAT if ever you feel stuck in some area of your life, if ever you feel life has lost its magic, if ever you wonder what on earth you are here for, or if you have a sense of your specialness but do not know how to tap this, consider looking for a guide in personal growth and potential. The Native American medicine wheel, vision quest, and purification/sweat lodge are catalysts for this. In our Western culture there are many models for personal growth and development offered by therapists trained in the different disciplines which can help one to become who one really is. Below, I suggest some places to find practical pointers in this. Just remember that your intention is what counts, and the quality of your intention will draw people, magazines and books, or other forms of information to you when you give it your commitment.

BOOKS ON NATIVE AMERICAN WISDOM

Anasazi – Ancient People of the Rock, Images of America Series.
Bahti, Mark and Tom, *Southwestern Indian Ceremonials*, K.C. Publications.
Bopp, Julie and Michael, Brown, Lee and Lane, Phil, *The Sacred Tree*, Four Worlds Development Press.
Brown, Joseph Epes, *Black Elk's the Sacred Pipe*, Normay & London, University of Oklahoma Press.

Bruchac, Joseph, *The Native American Sweat Lodge – History & Legends*, The Crossing Press, CA.

Foster, Steven, with Little Meredith and Sun Bear, *The Book of the Vision Quest*, Prentice Hall Press, NY.

Gifford, Eli and Cook, R. Michael, ed. *How Can One Sell the Air? Chief Seattle's Vision*, Book Publishing Company, Summertown, Tenn.

Hultkrantz, Ake, *Native Religions of North America*, Harper, San Francisco.

Ingerman, Sandra, *Soul Retrieval*, Harper, San Francisco.

Locke, Raymond Friday, *The Book of the Navajo*, Mankind, LA.

Lorler, Marie-Lu, *Shamanic Healing Within the Medicine Wheel*, Brotherhood of Life, Alberquerque.

Marquis, Arnold, *A Guide to America's Indians – Ceremonial, Reservations & Museums*, University of Oklahoma Press.

Nitch, Twylah, *Native Voice*, Seneca Indian Historical Society, NY.

Nitsch, Twylah, *Language of the Trees – A Seneca Indian Earthwalk*, Seneca Indian Historical Society, NY.

Nitsch, Twylah, *Language of the Stones*, Seneca Indian Historical Society, NY

Nitsch, Twylah, *Entering into the Silence – The Seneca Way*, Seneca Indian Historical Society, NY.

Rael, Joseph E., *Beautiful Painted Arrow*, Element, Shaftesbury.

Rael/Marlow, *Being & Vibration*, Council Oak Books, Tulsa, OK.

Ross Dr, A.C., *Mitakuye Oyasin*, Bear, Kyle, SD.

Sams, Jamie, *The Thirteen Original Clan Mothers*, Harper, San Francisco.

Sams, Jamie, *Earth Medicine* Harper San Francisco.

Sams, Jamie and Nitsch, Twylah, *Other Council Fires Were Here Before Ours*, Harper, San Francisco.

Storm, Hyemeyohsts, *Seven Arrows*, Ballantine Books, NY.

Sun, Bear, Wabun Wind and Mulligan, Crysalis, *Dancing With the Wheel – the Medicine Wheel Workbook*, Simon & Schuster.

Suzuki, David and Knudtson, Peter, *Wisdom of the Elders – Sacred Native Stories of Nature*, Bantam Books, NY.

Swanton, John R., *Indian Tribes of North America*, Smithsonian Institution Press, Washington & London.

Versluis, Arthur, *Native American Traditions*, Element, Shaftesbury.

Walker, Steven L., *The Southwest – a Pictorial History of the Land & its People*, Camelback Canyonlands Venture.

Wallace, Paul A.W., *The White Roots of Peace*, University of Pennsylvania Press.

Weatherford, Jack, *Indian Givers*, Fawcett Columbine, NY.

White Deer of Autumn, *The Native American Book of Life*, Beyond Words Publishing Inc., Hillsborough, Or.

White Deer of Autumn, *The Native American Book of Change*, Beyond Words Publishing Inc., Hillsborough, Or.

White, Jon Manchip, *Everyday Life of the North American Indian*, Indian Head Books, NY.

Ywahoo, Dhyani, *Voices of Our Ancestors*, Shambhala, Boston & London.

BOOKS WITH CARDS ON SELF-DISCOVERY

Sams, Jamie, *The Sacred Path Cards – The Discovery of the Self Through Native Teachings*, Harper, San Francisco.

Sams, Jamie and Carson, David, *The Medicine Cards*, Bear & Co.

Fire Lame Deer, Chief Archie and Sarkis, Helene, *The Lakota Sweat Lodge Cards – Spiritual Teachings of the Sioux*, Destiny Books, Rochester Vi.

Lerner, Isha and Mark, *Inner Child Cards, a Journey into Fairy Tales, Myth & Nature*, illus. Guilfoil, Christopher Bear, Santa Fe.

BOOKS TO GET STARTED ON PERSONAL GROWTH

Assagioli, Roberto M.D., *Psychosynthesis*, Turnstone Press, London.

Bond, Jean, *Behind the Masks*, Gateway Books, Bath.

Caddy, Eileen and Platts, David Earl, *Bringing More Love into Your Life: the Choice is Yours*, Findhorn Press, Forres.

Capacchione, Lucia, *The Creative Journal*, Newcastle Publishing Co. Inc, CA.

Ferrucci, Piero, *What We May Be*, Turnstone Press, London.

Garnett, Lynne, *Finding the Great Creative You*, Aslan Boulder Creek, CA.

Houston, Jean, *Life Force*, Dell, NY.

Houston, Jean, *Mind Games*, Turnstone Press, London.

Houston, Jean, *The Possible Human*, J.P. Tarcher, LA.

Karpinski, Gloria, *Where Two Worlds Touch*, Rider, London.

Price, John Randolph, *The Angels Within Us*, Fawcett Columbine, NY.

Rainer, Tristine, *The New Diary*, Angus & Robertson, London.

Rosanoff, Nancy, *Intuition Workout*, Aslan, Boulder Creek, CA.

Sams, Jamie, *The Thirteen Original Clan Mothers*, Harper San Francisco.

Sams, Jamie, *The Sacred Path Workbook*, Harper San Francisco.

Taylor, Cathryn L., *The Inner Child Workbook*, Tarcher/Perigee, NY.

Whitmore, Diana, *Psychosynthesis in Education*, Turnstone Press, London.

TAPES

Brown, Joseph Epes, *Black Elk: the Sacred Pipe*, read by Fred Contreras; Audio Literature. CA.

Mails, Thomas E., *Secret Native American Pathways*, Council Oak Books, Tulsa, OK.

Rael, Joseph, *Ancient Wisdom – Native American Teachings*, Council Oak Books, Tulsa, OK.

Sun Bear, *Vision of the Medicine Wheel*, Four Directions Productions.

DEALING WITH GRIEF

Ward, Barbara, *Healing Grief*, Vermilion, London.

Colgrove, Melba, Bloomfield, Harold H. and McWilliams, Peter, *How to Survive the Loss of a Love*, Prelude Press, CA.

UK MAGAZINES DEALING WITH PERSONAL GROWTH

Caduceus
Kindred Spirit
One Earth
Resurgence
Sacred Hoop
Human Potential

UK CENTRES DEALING WITH PERSONAL GROWTH

Findhorn Community, Findhorn, Forres IV36 OTZ, Scotland.
Gaunts House, Wimborne, Dorset.
Grimstone Community, Grimstone Manor, Yelverton, Devon PL20 7QY.
Hazlewood House, Loddiswell, Nr. Kingsbridge, S. Devon TQ7 4EB
Monkton Wild Court, Charmouth, Bridport, Dorset DT6 6DQ.
Pegasus Foundation, Runnings Park, Croft Bank, West Malvern, Worcs. WR14 4BP.
Psychosynthesis & Education Trust, 92/94 Tooley St., London SE1 2TH.
University of Avalon, The Courtyard, Glastonbury Experience, 2–4 High St., Glastonbury, Somerset BA6 9DU.